PICTURE YOURSELF
PLAYING BASS

Mike Chiavaro

Course Technology PTR

A part of Cengage Learning

COURSE TECHNOLOGY
CENGAGE Learning

Australia, Brazil, Japan, Korea, Mexico, Singapore, Spain, United Kingdom, United States

COURSE TECHNOLOGY
CENGAGE Learning™

Picture Yourself Playing Bass
Mike Chiavaro

Publisher and General Manager,
Course Technology PTR:
Stacy L. Hiquet

Associate Director of Marketing:
Sarah Panella

Manager of Editorial Services:
Heather Talbot

Marketing Manager:
Mark Hughes

Acquisitions Editor:
Orren Merton

Project/Copy Editor:
Kezia Endsley

Technical Reviewer:
Barry Wood

PTR Editorial Services Coordinator:
Jen Blaney

Interior Layout:
Shawn Morningstar

Cover Designer:
Mike Tanamachi

Indexer:
Broccoli Creative Services

Proofreader:
Carolyn Keating

Printed in the United States of America
1 2 3 4 5 6 7 12 11 10 09

For product information and technology assistance, contact us at

Cengage Learning Customer and Sales Support,
1-800-354-9706

For permission to use material from this text or product, submit all requests online at
cengage.com/permissions

Further permissions questions can be emailed to
permissionrequest@cengage.com

Library of Congress Control Number: 2008929231
ISBN-13: 978-1-59863-508-9
ISBN-10: 1-59863-508-5

Course Technology
25 Thomson Place
Boston, MA 02210
USA

Cengage Learning is a leading provider of customized learning solutions with office locations around the globe, including Singapore, the United Kingdom, Australia, Mexico, Brazil, and Japan. Locate your local office at:
international.cengage.com/region

Cengage Learning products are represented in Canada by Nelson Education, Ltd.

For your lifelong learning solutions, visit **courseptr.com**
Visit our corporate website at **cengage.com**

This book is dedicated to my parents,
Ron and Cathy Chiavaro.

Without your constant support,
this book never would have happened.

Acknowledgments

Thanks to:

My brother, Rob. It's crazy to think that you're all grown up and bigger than I am.

Johnny Mac, for being my musical mentor. You're the best teacher I've ever had.

Grey Mcmurray and Ryan Ferreira. Not only are you both amazing friends, you are the two best musicians that I know.

Theo Wargo, for taking amazing pictures for this book and helping out with the DVD.

Rich Russano, for changing your flight to stay in New York and film this DVD.

Jon Elsas, for being my #1 guy through all these years.

Sean Riback; no one can make me laugh like you do.

Joe Bagale, for keeping it on the one.

Rob and Judi, Kathy and John, and Jackie and Michael for your constant support.

Ed RosenBerg, just for having a mustache.

Chris Pressler, for providing a video camera on such short notice.

And of course, Erin. The time that we've spent together has been nothing short of amazing for me. I'm so lucky to have met you.

About the Author

MIKE CHIAVARO can be found playing all over New York City with groups such as Knights on Earth, Jerseyband, Bell, Burlap to Cashmere, Bacci, Amy Lynn and the Gunshow, The Keith Ward Group, The Christine Hagan Project, and Dave Crowell's Naked Brunch. He has worked as a session musician for a lineup of legendary producers including Phil Ramone (Paul Simon and Bill Joel), Jack Douglas (Aerosmith and John Lennon), Brian Harding (Jennifer Lopez and Dream Theater), Anthony J. Resta (Collective Soul and Duran Duran), Anthony Winters, and John Hill. Touring credits include several national tours with Czech Grammy Winner Lenka Dusilova, Bob America, and James Harries. A graduate of the Eastman School of Music, Mike has also performed and/or recorded with Danielle Evin, Nell Bryden, Spencer Day, Rose Falcon, Tamarama, Courtney Drummey, Dave Truet's Clarify, Paul Cox, Neos Ensemble, and Megumi Kanda. His endorsements include Ashdown Amplification and Clifford Roi Basses.

Table of Contents

Introduction

THE ELECTRIC BASS IS PERHAPS the most understated instrument in rock and pop music. Being a bass player isn't necessarily about being flashy or upfront on stage, it's about providing the rhythmic and harmonic foundation for the music. Traditionally, the bass plays a supportive role in a band. As a part of the rhythm section, the bass player and the drummer are expected to lock into a feel or groove. In addition to that, the bass also has the responsibility of outlining the harmony along with the chordal instruments and the singer.

A good bass player has the power to turn a decent band into a great band. This book is designed for the beginner bass student and will cover all of the main points on how to become a great, solid, functional bass player. Every topic is explored, including how to buy a bass, keeping the rhythm, understanding harmony, reading music, and how to practice effectively. The book even includes some specialty, non-traditional bass techniques such as slap bass, tapping, and muting techniques. You will start from the bottom and work your way to the top. By the end of this book, you will be prepared to tackle almost any musical situation.

What You'll Find in This Book

After reading this book, you will know how to do the following:

▶ Choose a bass and accessories that are right for your specific needs and playing style.

▶ Tune your bass quickly and effectively.

▶ Use proper hand techniques without creating stress or tension in your hands.

▶ Use both hands to maximize your bass playing.

▶ Read music and use a tablature.

▶ Understand the importance of the modes and modal fingerings.

▶ Understand the major and minor scales, including arpeggios and inversions.

▶ Practice with a metronome.

▶ Know how to ear train by yourself or with a friend.

▶ Use a pick with your bass for specialty sounds.

▶ Understand what slap bass is.

▶ Use the DVD to practice and fine-tune your bass sounds.

The book will be helpful to newbies who have never played any instrument in the past as well as players of other instruments who are now ready to take the plunge to the bass guitar.

How This Book Is Organized

This book contains nine chapters and two appendixes:

CHAPTER 1: "Getting Started: What You Need to Start Playing the Electric Bass." This chapter starts by discussing how to pick a bass and amplifier that meet your needs and tastes, including whether you should start with a four-string bass or a five-string one. You'll also learn all about pickups and learn how to properly tune your bass. At the end of this chapter, you'll plug in and play your very first exercise, with an accompanying example on the DVD.

CHAPTER 2: "Note Names, Your Hands, and the Importance of Good Technique." This chapter teaches you how to properly memorize the note names and frets. It discusses the difference between the plucking hand and the fingering hand. You'll learn in this chapter how to hold the bass properly, with a tension-free wrist. In the last part of this chapter, you'll learn to use the C major scale and play some new exercises (which you can also see on the DVD).

CHAPTER 3: "Reading Music." This chapter is dedicated to teaching you all the note names. It discusses the staff, the Bass clef, what time signatures and measures are, and what accidentals are. A good deal of this chapter is devoted to practice exercises that can help you learn the notes and strings on the staff. The best way to learn to read music is through practice, and you can return to the exercises in this chapter as much as you need to in order to learn to read. All the exercises are on the DVD as well.

CHAPTER 4: "The Blues and Major Scales in Other Keys." This chapter covers the history of the Blues and discusses the 12-bar Blues form as well as other Blues bass lines. You'll learn the Blues scale and the notes typically associated with the Blues sound. Through many exercises and DVD guidance, you'll learn how to play the Blues!

CHAPTER 5: "The Modes." In this chapter, you learn all about the modes, which is a type of scale. You'll learn and play several types of modes, including Lyndian, Mixolydian, Aeolian, and Locrian. Each mode has a different sound or tonal structure and by learning the modes and practicing them through the exercises in this chapter, you'll be adding to your repertoire of knowledge.

CHAPTER 6: "Intervals and Ear Training." An interval is the difference in pitch between two notes. Knowing the intervals and how to play them is an important component to being a good bass player. This chapter also addresses a very important aspect of music called ear training. Being able to play your instrument will only get you so far. Being able to hear and identify what you or others are playing is equally, if not more, valuable.

CHAPTER 7: "Specialty Techniques." This entire chapter is dedicated to special bass techniques such as slap bass, popping, hammering, and tapping. These techniques are fun to hear and see, but they can be a challenge to learn and master. This chapter's exercises will help you do just that.

CHAPTER 8: "Minor Scales and Intervals." Up to this point, the book has been dedicated to the C major scale. Now that you have a handle on that scale, it's time to move on to the minor scales. This chapter covers all the minor scales and intervals, with exercises to help you put it all together.

CHAPTER 9: "Harmony: Playing and Understanding Chords." This chapter deals with and explains harmony so that you can begin to play with and understand other players' chords (three or more notes played at the same time) when they show you their latest. You'll play a C major chord, an F major chord, a G major chord, and more. You'll also learn what major and minor double stops are, and how to use chords and harmonics to take your playing to the next level.

IN APPENDIX A, you'll see a list of the top 20 most influential bass players as I see it. This is a good place to go when you need some inspiration, since one of the best ways to become better at the bass is to listen to great bass players.

IN APPENDIX B, the Glossary, you'll find all the important terms and concepts discussed throughout the book in one convenient area, so when you forget what the "circle of fifths" is, for example, you can look it up quickly.

About the DVD

When you see the DVD icon, it means that the accompanying DVD contains tutorials related to the discussion or topic being covered.

Now let me give you a word of advice about how to use the DVD properly. The best way to internalize the lessons in this book is to start with the text. Take your time and make sure that you fully understand the topics before you watch the DVD. Once you've played through the examples and feel confident with the material covered, you should use the DVD to check yourself.

Don't rush, though. Some of these lessons will take a while to grasp. It's better to go slow and learn these things the right way. Jeff Campbell, my bass teacher in college, used to say, "practice makes permanent." Practicing is a great thing, just as long as you're practicing the right way. If you play an exercise the wrong way 100 times, you're just developing bad habits and wasting your time. There's nothing wrong with going slow and steady. Good luck and have fun with it!

Getting Started:
What You Need
to Start Playing the

Electric Bass

THERE ARE ONLY A FEW NECESSARY items that you need to start playing the electric bass. All of these things can be purchased for a relatively small amount of money, if you're willing to shop around a little bit. In this chapter, I give you tips on how to find a good bass and amplifier that work for you. Keep in mind that purchasing expensive equipment at this point is not necessary. For a beginner's purposes, you should look for a solid bass that will hold up for a long time without needing repair. Once the equipment is taken care of, you'll learn the names of the different parts of the bass and get plugged in and playing for the first time.

Choosing a Bass and Amplifier

THIS IS AN EXCITING STEP in your quest to play the electric bass. For your purposes here, any bass will do for now. If Mom or Dad has an old bass lying around in the basement, use that. If you see an old, funky-looking bass at a garage sale for $20, grab it. Otherwise, take a trip to a local guitar shop. There are plenty of good, new basses for under $200. A few brands that I recommend for an inexpensive bass with decent parts are Yamaha, Ibanez, and Squire. Some shops even offer beginner packs that include a bass and an amplifier together. Like I said, spending a lot of money is not necessary at this point. You can purchase more expensive basses later, after you've built a solid musical foundation.

Your First Bass

There are three main characteristics to consider when purchasing an inexpensive bass: *The number of strings* it has, the *size of the neck*, and the *sound possibilities* of the bass. Let's take a closer look at these three options.

Number of Strings

I would advise you to start with a *four-string bass*. The first electric bass that was introduced in the early 1950s had four strings. Most bass players find that sufficient. It wasn't until many years later that people started making five- or six-string basses to extend the range of notes for the instrument.

As a beginner bass player it is important that you build your foundation on a four-string bass. Once you grasp a few main concepts, you might want to consider upgrading to a bass that has more strings. But for right now, remember that some of the greatest music of all time was played or recorded with a four-string bass—look at Paul McCartney, James Jamerson, Jaco Pastorius, or Sting, and the list goes on and on. Check out how many strings your favorite bass player has. Figure 1.1 shows what a four-string bass looks like.

Neck Size

Some basses are made with smaller necks and some with larger ones. By this I am referring to the thickness of the neck, not how many frets it has. The size of your hands should play a role in this decision. I advise you to try out a bunch of different-size basses before making your decision. Keep in mind that your hands will learn to stretch out after a little bit of practice, but you want something that feels somewhat comfortable from the start.

Sound Possibilities

All basses sound different, which is one exciting aspect of choosing a bass. Now the big question is, why do they sound different? Well, there are a few main factors that contribute to this. String type, the amp you're using, and even your fingers will have an impact on the sound of a bass. However, one huge factor is the pickup configuration.

Figure 1.1
The four-string bass

Pickups capture the vibrations of the strings and send those vibrations to your amplifier. Some common bass pickup types are precision, or "P," pickups and jazz, or "J," pickups. A "P" pickup configuration (displayed in Figure 1.2) consists of two small pickups offset slightly along the length of the body of the bass. Notice that each pickup is placed beneath two strings.

Figure 1.2
The "P" pickup configuration

The "J" pickup configuration (displayed in Figure 1.3) consists of two longer pickups that are spaced farther apart. The pickup closest to the bridge of the bass is referred to as the *bridge* or *back* pickup. The pickup closest to the neck of the bass is referred to as the *neck* or *front* pickup. Notice that each "J" pickup spans all four strings of the bass, while each "P" pickup spans two strings.

Figure 1.3
The "J" pickup configuration

Generally, P-style pickups are used in rock music and J-style pickups are used in jazz or fusion music. However, this rule is broken all the time. Plenty of rock bass players use jazz-style pickups, and although it is a little less common, there are jazz players who use P-style pickups. The best way to figure out which sound you prefer is to try both types. There is no wrong or right decision when it comes to pickups; it's all a matter of personal preference. Some basses even come with both types of pickups.

Another, more rare, type of bass pickup is the *humbucker.* The humbucker is similar in length to the jazz-style pickup but is roughly double the width. This type of pickup is usually found in newer, more modern-sounding basses, and tends to be louder than a standard jazz or precision pickup.

Now that you know about all of these options, it's a good time to go out and actually play a few basses with different pickups and see which you prefer. Tell the person at the music shop that you want to hear the difference between a jazz-style bass and a precision-style bass.

Your First Amplifier

You will need a bass amplifier in order to hear yourself clearly. Don't worry; just like the bass, you won't need to spend a lot of money on your first amp. Right now you're just looking for a small practice amp that will produce a little bit of sound. Anywhere from 15–50 watts should be plenty. Here are a few things to consider when buying your first amp.

Watts

What is a *watt*, you ask? Think about it like this: A watt refers to power. The higher the wattage, the more power the amp has. More power equals more volume. A 15- to 30-watt amp is ideal for practicing alone in your room. A 50-watt amp produces enough power or volume to start playing with a band in a small venue. An amp with 200–500 watts is used for bigger situations, such as playing in a club in front of a few hundred people.

Combo Amps vs. Separate Amp Head and Speaker Cabinet

Another factor to consider when buying a bass amp is the difference between a combo amp and a separate amp head and speaker cabinet. The distinction is simple. All bass amplifiers consist of two main components—an amp head and a speaker cabinet. The amp head is the part that you plug your bass into.

This component contains all of the electronics and needs to be plugged into an outlet to receive power. There are several knobs on the front of it for altering the sound of the amp. See Figure 1.4.

Figure 1.4
The amp head

The speaker cabinet is the enclosure that holds the speakers. This is the component that the sound actually comes out of. Bass speakers generally range in size from 8–18 inches. See Figure 1.5.

Figure 1.5
Speaker cabinet

A *combo amp* means that the amp head and speaker cabinet are already connected in one enclosure. Combo amps generally have lower wattage and are less expensive than buying a separate amp head and speaker cabinet. For right now, I suggest you keep it simple and get yourself an inexpensive combo amp. Some reliable brands to check out are:

Gallien-Krueger www.gallien-krueger.com
Hartke www.samsontech.com/products/brandpage.cfm?brandID=3
Fender www.fender.com
Roland www.rolandus.com

Speaker Size

Do you need big speakers to have a big sound? The answer is no. Bass speakers come in a variety of sizes. Smaller speakers produce a tighter, more focused sound, whereas bigger speakers produce a warmer, thicker sound. Many bass players use a combination of speaker sizes to achieve their desired sound. One common configuration for larger bass amps is to have one 15" speaker in the bottom cabinet and four 10" speakers in the top cabinet. This way you can get a warm, thick sound from the 15" speaker while maintaining clarity with the four 10" speakers. When buying your amp, take a few minutes to test out different speaker sizes so you can hear the difference. Do you prefer the sound of bigger or smaller speakers?

Check out the DVD When You See This Icon

Anytime you see this DVD icon in the margin during the course of this book, it means that the current discussion or explanation has a DVD component to it. Pop the DVD in your player to go through the discussion step by step. Hands-on is the best way to learn the bass!

Three Useful Accessories

NOW THAT YOU HAVE A GRASP of what to look for when purchasing your first electric bass and amplifier, let's take a brief look at some useful accessories. One thing that is essential is a ¼" *cable*. This cable, which is used to connect your bass to the amplifier, varies in length, quality, and price. The average price for a cable like this should be somewhere around $15. Second on the list of accessories is a *tuner*. This device will help you get each of the strings on your bass perfectly in tune; it's a must. Tuners start at around $20, and any brand will do for now. Another useful tool is a *music stand*. Technically, you could rest your music on a table or chair, but that can get annoying and will ultimately give you neck cramps from hunching over. Music stands are cheap and they will improve your posture. A nice accessory to put on your music stand is a *blank manuscript notebook*. This will help you track your progress and remember what your bass teacher showed you in your lessons. Not only that, but a music notebook will also allow you to write down and keep track of any musical ideas you have. Finally, last but not least is a *strap*. A strap will hold your bass at the perfect height. This is an important piece of equipment because it ensures that your bass is always resting in the same place against your body, whether you're sitting down or standing up.

Chapter 1

Electric Bass Diagram

BEFORE YOU GO ANY FURTHER, let's take a look at the names of the different parts on the electric bass. As the book goes on, I refer to these parts often in this book. Figure 1.6 gives you a diagram to help you visualize what's what.

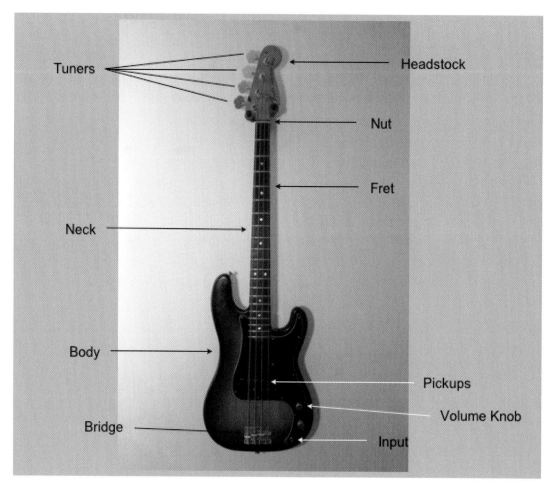

Figure 1.6
Electric bass diagram

Tuning Your Bass

YOU SHOULD TUNE YOUR bass every time you pick up your instrument. Basses and guitars go out of tune easily, and your instrument needs to be in tune in order for it to sound good. All tuners look and work a little differently (see Figure 1.7), but they all do the same thing—get your instrument in tune. The goal here is to tune each of the four strings to their specific pitch. The names of the open strings, starting with the thickest (fourth) string and going to the thinnest (first) string, are *E, A, D,* and *G.*

Now plug your bass into the input of the tuner using your ¼" cable. Make sure that your volume knob is turned all the way up. Turn the tuner on and play the thickest (fourth) open string and let it ring. Playing an open string means that you don't push down on any of the frets with your fingering hand. This note should read **E** on the tuner. There will be flashing lights on either side of the note, telling you whether that string is sharp or flat in pitch. If the flashing light is to the left side of the note, the string is flat. Turn the E string tuning peg counter-clockwise to bring the pitch higher or sharp. If the flashing light is to the right side of the note, that means that the string is sharp, and you want to turn the tuning peg clockwise to bring the pitch down or flat. Small turns can have a big effect on the pitch, so start off slowly. When you're done tuning, make sure that you turn your tuner off. See "Tuning" on the DVD to watch me tune my bass.

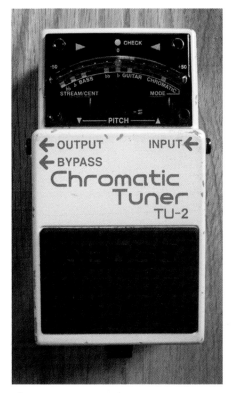

Figure 1.7
A standard guitar/bass tuner

Plugging In for the First Time

NOW THAT YOUR BASS is in tune, you're ready to start playing. First, plug your amplifier into an outlet and make sure that the power switch is set to off. Now plug one end of the ¼" cable into the input jack of your amplifier. Plug the other end of the cable into the input on your bass. (Refer back to Figure 1.6 if you are unsure of where that is.) Once both ends are plugged in, make sure that the volume knob on your amplifier is turned all the way down, or as far counterclockwise as it will go. Now is a good time to make sure that the volume knob on your bass is turned up. Turn the power button on the amplifier to the on position, and gradually turn up the volume until you can hear your bass through the amp. You'll probably notice that there are some other knobs on the amplifier in addition to volume. Depending upon what kind of bass amp you have, these knobs will vary. The most common knobs are *bass*, *mid*, and *treble*. These will help you shape the sound of the instrument by adding or subtracting specific frequencies. For right now, turn those three knobs to the 12 o'clock position.

The first thing that you're going to try is a warm-up exercise. This will help you stretch out your hands and release some tension. I recommend doing this right after you tune your bass, each and every time that you play. Remember, your hands are delicate and you don't want to overuse them. So if your fingers start to feel uncomfortable, take a break or move on to something else. You should only have to spend a few minutes a day on this exercise for it to be effective. It's simple.

Warm-up Exercise

Okay, in this exercise all that you're going to do is play the first five notes on the low E (fourth) string. Start by playing the open E string, now play the first fret with your index finger, the second fret with your middle finger, the third fret with your ring finger, and the fourth fret with your pinky (see Figure 1.8).

Make sure to pluck each note with the index or middle finger of your plucking (right) hand. The goal is to play very slowly and to use minimal movement with your fingering hand. When you press down on the second fret with your middle finger, try to keep your index finger as close to the first fret as possible.

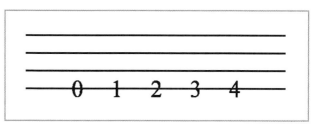

Figure 1.8
Tablature for warm-up exercise

Think of it as assigning each finger to a fret. Even if you're not playing that specific fret, you want to keep its assigned finger as close to it as possible. The same thing goes when you're pressing down on the third fret with your ring finger; your index and middle fingers should be close to the first and second frets, slightly pushing down.

Finally, when you press down on the fourth fret with your pinky, all four of your fingers should be slightly pressing down on each fret. Using the fingers that are not playing the note will provide strength to your weaker fingers like your ring finger and pinky.

Tablature

Tablature is an easy way to read music. The four lines that you see represent the four strings of the bass from the lowest to the highest. The numbers shown on the strings tell you which fret to play. For instance, a number three on the lowest line means you play the third fret on the E, or lowest, string.

Just as a test, try pressing down on the fourth fret on any string with your pinky and keep your other three fingers raised up. Notice the amount of force you need to use. Now press those three fingers down over the first three frets and push down on the fourth fret again with your pinky. Because your other fingers are helping out, you don't need to push down nearly as hard. See Figure 1.9 for correct placement of your fingers.

Figure 1.9
This is the way your hand should look when pressing down on the fourth fret with your pinky

Once you get the hang of this process, try the same exercise on each of the other three strings. Play the open string, followed by the first four frets on that string. Remember to assign a finger to each fret and to keep your fingers down. Once you get up to the fourth fret on the G string, play the whole exercise backwards. Start on the fourth fret of the G string and go all the way down to the open E string.

Your First Bass Line

YOUR FIRST BASS LINE is going to be a classic one. It's the theme song to *Peter Gunn,* which was a television show that aired from 1958–1961. Written by Henry Mancini, this bluesy bass line is very memorable. The whole thing is played on one string, the low E. I show it to you in Figure 1.10.

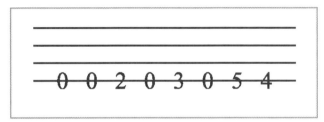

Figure 1.10
Tablature for the theme to *Peter Gunn*

Just as before, I want you to assign a different finger to each fret. So the second fret will be played with your index finger, the third fret with your middle finger, the fourth fret with your ring finger, and the fifth fret with your pinky. This will cut down on unnecessary movement with your fingering hand. Also, when you're plucking remember to alternate between your index and middle fingers. Take it slow and try to make all of the notes sound even.

Note Names, Your Hands, and the Importance of

Good Technique

AVING GOOD TECHNIQUE can only help you. Technique is certainly not something that you need to think about while you're playing; it's something that you think about while you're practicing. There is a difference. If you practice your bass a certain way, these habits will emerge when you're playing. Technique is something that you gradually build up over time. You will save yourself a ton of time and frustration if you learn how to play the bass correctly from the beginning, as opposed to developing bad habits early on and realizing later that you have to change them. Believe me, I developed a few bad habits when I started playing the bass—trying to unlearn those habits was tough. Besides, it's actually easier to play with good technique. People call it "good" or "proper" technique because it works. People have been developing electric bass technique for over 50 years. That means that you don't have to go through the trial-and-error process the same way they did. Playing correctly also helps you avoid hand injuries, such as tendonitis. In this chapter, I show you the correct way to use both of your hands. Also, get ready to learn your first scale, as well as a really fun new warm-up exercise. But first, it's time to learn a few note names.

Memorizing Note Names

T HE NEXT STEP for you is to learn the names of the notes on the bass. You learned in the last chapter about the four open strings. Starting with the thickest string and going to the thinnest, the names of the four open strings are E, A, D, and G. Come up with a phrase that will help you memorize these, such as *E*ddie *A*te *D*elicious *G*rapes.

Now that you know the string names, you're ready to move on to the notes of the first four frets of each string. See Figure 2.1.

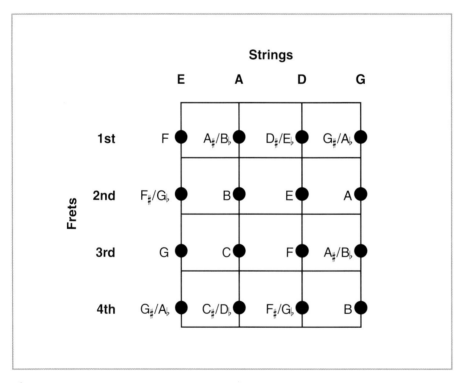

Figure 2.1
Note names, frets 1 through 4

The only way to learn the names of the notes on your instrument is to memorize them. I suggest working on them one string at a time. The best way to do that is to say the name of the notes as you play them. So, play the open E string and literally say "E" in your head. Then play the first fret on the E string and say "F," play the second fret on the E string and say "F♯/G♭," and so on. Spend a day on each string and before you know it you'll have the first four frets of the bass down. Make sure to put in the time needed to learn these note names before you continue.

Why Do Some of the Notes Have Two Names?

When a note has two names, such as F♯/G♭, they both refer to the same musical pitch, which is called the *enharmonic equivalent.* That just means that the two notes sound identical in pitch. For example, the notes F♯ and G♭ are enharmonically equivalent. They are really the same pitch with two different names. The note name you choose for the pitch depends on what key the music is in. Figure 2.2 shows how it looks.

Figure 2.2
The note F♯/G♭

Your Hands

NOW IT'S TIME TO LEARN how to properly hold the bass. Obviously, you have two hands, which are going to play equally valuable roles in this process. You have a *plucking hand,* which is the hand that you're going to be plucking the strings with, and you have a *fingering hand,* which you will use to press down the notes on the fingerboard of the bass. For you righties out there, your right hand will be the plucking hand, and your left the fingering hand. If you're a lefty, you're going to flip those instructions. Don't forget to check out the DVD when you see this icon.

The Plucking Hand

In this section, I'm going to help you find a good location for your plucking hand. A general point to remember is that the closer you pluck toward the bridge, the more defined or clear a note is going to sound. When you pluck closer to the neck or fingerboard of the bass, you will get a much warmer, fatter sound. See Figures 2.3 and 2.4.

Figure 2.3
Plucking close to the bridge will give you a clear, defined sound

Figure 2.4
Plucking close to the neck will give you a warm, round sound

Try playing the warm-up exercise from Chapter 1 with your plucking hand in different positions on the bass. Moving your hand just a few inches will make a big difference in the way the notes sound. A very common place to leave your plucking hand on your bass is right over a pickup. When you think about it, the pickup is capturing the sound of your strings, so playing close to it can give you a nice, full sound. The edge of the pickup can also be a great spot for you to rest your thumb while you're playing. This can give you really good leverage, too. See Figure 2.5.

Figure 2.5
You can use the pickup as a resting spot for your thumb

Thumb Muting Technique

A common problem for beginner bass players is keeping quiet the strings that are not being played. To solve this problem, we'll take a look at an easy string-muting technique. There are several string-muting techniques, but I find the *moving thumb* approach to be the simplest and most effective. What you're going to do is use the thumb on your plucking hand (the right hand if you're right-handed) to mute the strings that are behind the one that is actually being played. For instance, if I'm playing on the G string, the tip of my thumb will be resting on the D string and the side of my thumb will be touching the A and E strings. Now if I'm playing on the D string, my thumb is resting on the A string, with the side of my thumb touching the E string. If I'm playing on the A string, my thumb is resting on the E string, and finally if I'm playing on the E string, my thumb is resting on the side of the pickup.

Figure 2.6
Using the strings as a resting spot for your thumb

Not only does this help you mute the strings that aren't being played, it also helps you maintain a consistent hand position. Here's a really easy way to practice this technique. Go back to the first warm-up exercise from Chapter 1, where you played the first five notes on each string. You're going to do the same thing again, except this time you're going to start on the G string and work your way backwards. Keep track of where your thumb is and make sure to alternate between your index and middle fingers when plucking. Notice the position of those two fingers in Figure 2.6.

Alternate Your Fingers

Alternating between your index and middle fingers when you pluck is a good habit to get into. The most basic reason being that you're splitting the amount of work in half. Why not give your fingers a break? Not only will you avoid stress and tension in your plucking hand, but I also guarantee that you'll be able to play longer and faster in the end. Practice being efficient and make sure to alternate.

When alternating between your index and middle fingers, try to keep track of the other fingers on your plucking hand. Ideally, you want them to stay down. For some reason your pinky will probably have a tendency to want to stick up or out. Be aware of it and try to keep it down.

Avoid Bending Your Wrist

One really bad habit that I see all the time with beginner bass students is that they tend to bend the wrist of their plucking hand. What you want to do is keep your wrist straight. I'll show you why. First, bend your wrist forward and try to alternate your index and middle fingers repeatedly. That probably doesn't feel great, does it? Now straighten your wrist out and do the same thing. It becomes so much easier. There's way less stress and tension involved. Make it easier on yourself, and keep your wrist straight. See Figure 2.7.

Figure 2.7
A straight, tension-free wrist

The Fingering Hand

Now I'm going to talk a little bit about how you want to position your fingering hand (the left hand if you're right-handed). As discussed, it's helpful to think about assigning four fingers to a set of four frets. This is what's called a *position*. The reason for this is that you're preparing your four fingers to cover a lot of ground without a lot of movement. When you play, you want to try to move your fingering hand as little as possible. Try to keep your fingers down and close to the fretboard, even when they're not being used.

Your Thumb

The location of your thumb is extremely important when developing a good fingering hand. Generally, you want your thumb to be aligned with your middle finger. Think of the two as being a clamp. See Figure 2.8.

Figure 2.8
The clamp approach, whereby the thumb and middle finger act as a clamp

Keeping these two fingers together is helpful for a number of reasons. The main reason being that you'll maintain a good, consistent hand shape, which is crucial for when you move to some faster, more complex lessons.

Fingertips vs. Pads

When pressing down on a string, try to use the tips of your fingers. For one thing, it will force you to spread your fingers apart and help you avoid a closed-hand approach. Playing with a closed, bunched-up fingering hand is guaranteed to trip you up. When your fingers are spread apart you will have much greater facility on the instrument. Watch a great violinist or classical guitar player for examples of good fingertip technique.

A Tension-Free Wrist

Just as with your plucking hand, you want to avoid sharp angles with your fingering hand. The biggest contributor to this problem is the height of your bass. If you wear your bass too low or too high, you'll notice that your wrist automatically becomes bent at a sharper angle than normal. To fix this problem, you can simply adjust your strap so that your bass sits at a comfortable level. Figure 2.9 shows an example of what you don't want your wrist to look like.

Okay, now that you've read about all of these correct methods, try to be aware of them as you play. You should always be conscious of the shape and location of your hands while you are practicing. This way, you'll be in complete control of the sounds coming out of your instrument. To help you work on this awareness, I'm going to show you how to play your first scale.

Figure 2.9
Incorrect wrist position

C Major Scale

A *SCALE IS A SERIES OF NOTES* that differ in pitch according to a specific scheme. So basically, it's just a group of notes played in order. The C major scale is an extremely important element in music. It's the basis for almost everything in music. In order for you to take your music and bass playing to the next level, you have to know how a major scale works.

Let's play a C major scale so you can see what I'm talking about. I'll write it out in tablature for you in Figure 2.10.

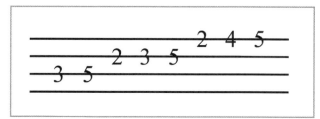

Figure 2.10
C major scale

Practicing the C Major Scale

Each time that you play through the C major scale you should say the names of the notes and the scale degree numbers as you play them.

Here's an easy way to play this. Start with your middle finger on the third fret of the A string, which is the note C. Now play these notes:

▶ **The fifth fret on the A string with your pinky. This note is D.**

▶ **The second fret on the D string with your index finger. This note is E.**

▶ **The third fret on the D string with your middle finger. This note is F.**

▶ **The fifth fret on the D string with your pinky. This note is G.**

▶ **The second fret on the G string with your index finger. This note is A.**

▶ **The fourth fret on the G string with your ring finger. This note is B.**

▶ **The fifth fret on the G string with your pinky. This note is C.**

Now think about the names of the notes that you just played: C, D, E, F, G, A, B, and C. Nice. No sharps or flats. That is a C major scale. Notice that there are a total of eight notes in the major scale (it's one octave). Another helpful thing to do is to apply numbers to the different notes, or intervals. These numbers relate to the *scale degrees.* For instance, C is 1, D is 2, E is 3, F is 4, and so on. This will make things easier when you move on to different keys.

Whole Steps and Half Steps

A major scale is made up of a combination of *whole steps* and *half steps.* A whole step is an interval of two semitones, and a half step is an interval of one semitone. Confused? On the most basic level, a whole step is the distance between two frets on your bass, and a half step (or semitone) is the distance between one fret. So play a C on the third fret of the A string. Now, go up one fret and play a D♭. That's a half step (one semitone).

Now play that C again and then go up two frets and play a D. That's a whole step (two semitones).

Okay, ready for the golden formula? A major scale is made up of this combination of whole and half steps: **whole, whole, half, whole, whole, whole, half.**

Permutations of Four

THIS NEXT EXERCISE will strengthen your hands in a short time. The goal is to play slowly and correctly. What you're going to do is look at a group of four frets, or a *position*. This exercise can be applied to any group of four frets on the bass, but for now you'll start with the first four. Remember, there are a lot of things to think about regarding proper hand placement, so I want you to take this next exercise slowly and really focus on one hand at a time. Practice makes permanent.

This exercise takes the first warm-up exercise to the next level. In the first exercise, you played the first four frets of the E string in a row. Let's keep that idea, but now each time that you go up to the next fret, also go to the next string. So start on the first fret of the E string, and then play the second fret on the A string, the third fret on the D string, and the fourth fret on the G string.

Once you get there, do the same thing backwards. Play the first fret on the G string, the second fret on the D string, the third fret on the A string, and the fourth fret on the E string. This pattern is called 1234, which refers to the fingers that you're using and the frets that you're playing. I'll lay it out for you in tablature (see Figure 2.11).

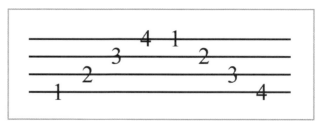

Figure 2.11
Permutations of four

When you finish that pattern, repeat it, but start on the second fret of the E string. So you'll play the second fret on the E string, the third fret on the A string, the fourth fret on the D string, and the fifth fret on the G string. Going backwards, you'll play the second fret on the G string, the third fret on the D string, the fourth fret on the A string, and the fifth fret on the E string. This is written out in Figure 2.12.

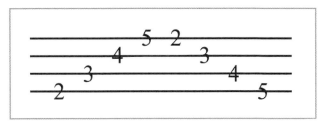

Figure 2.12
Permutations of four, starting on the second fret

Each time that you finish the pattern, you can start over one fret higher. Go all the way up the fretboard until you run out of notes. Once you feel comfortable with this exercise, you can make up your own permutation of four notes. The only rule is that you have to play each string in order, meaning EADG going up and GDAE going down. Just switch up the fret order.

One order that I like is 1324. So starting on the first fret, you would play the first fret on the E string, the third fret on the A string, the second fret on the D string, and the fourth fret on the G string. Going backwards, the first fret is on the G string, the third fret is on the D string, the second fret is on the A string, and the fourth fret is on the E string. See Figure 2.13.

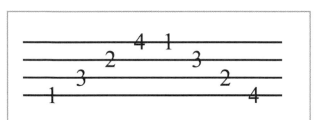

Figure 2.13
Permutations of four: 1324

The possibilities are almost endless. Once you find a few different combinations that you like, try playing one pattern going up and then a different pattern going down. Say, for instance, 1342 going up and 3421 going down. See Figure 2.14.

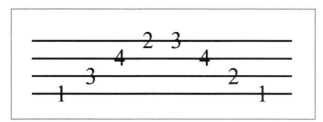

Figure 2.14
Permutations of four: 1342 up and 3421 down

This is guaranteed to make your fingers move in ways that they normally wouldn't. If you want to get really serious about it you can take the time to write out every possible combination of this group and work on a different pattern every few days. Try 1234, 1243, 1324, 1342, 1423, 1432, and so on. Remember that you don't always have to start on 1, either. When these patterns begin to get comfortable, try starting with a different finger. How about 2134 or 3241? Mix it up.

This exercise will do a lot for your bass playing. Aside from stretching out your hands and making your brain work really hard, it can be used as an avenue to work on your hands. Don't worry about playing these exercises fast; there's no need to. Play them at ridiculously slow tempos and teach your hands the correct way to play.

Review

ERE'S A LIST OF EVERYTHING that Chapter 2 covered regarding your hands. There's a lot of stuff to remember, so it's a good idea to take a quick glance over this list when you sit down to practice. Make sure that you're taking care of all these points:

The Plucking Hand

▶ Mute the strings that are not being played.

▶ Alternate your fingers when plucking.

▶ Keep your pinky down.

▶ Keep your wrist straight.

The Fingering Hand

▶ Line your thumb up with your middle finger (clamp).

▶ Play with the tips of your fingers.

▶ Avoid sharp wrist angles.

Reading

Music

L EARNING TO READ MUSIC IS LIKE learning another language. It's a way for musicians to communicate with each other. Why is this important? Well, here are a few reasons. First off, think about the possibility of opening a book and being able to play *any* style of music on your instrument. Want to learn how to play a Beatles song? Or how about a piece by Bach, or Metallica? What about jazz or the blues? There's no other way to have instant access to all styles of music. Not only that, but you'll be able to communicate with other musicians. You can sit down with a complete stranger and make music together, regardless of where you're from or what language you speak.

Reading music will also help you communicate on a much easier level. Right now there are general things I can tell you to play, but once you know how to read music, I can get specific with what notes I want you to play and how I want you to play them, which is really important for you to understand. Reading music will allow us to communicate in a much clearer and more detailed way. Let's get started; it's much easier than you think.

Finishing Up with Note Names

A T THIS POINT YOU should have a grasp of the names of the notes on the first four frets of each string. In order to read music, you're going to have to learn the rest of the notes on the bass. Let's start there.

Now let's move on to frets 5 through 8 (see Figure 3.1). Don't feel overwhelmed. You'll notice that once you start memorizing the notes, you'll learn little tricks and patterns to help you along the way.

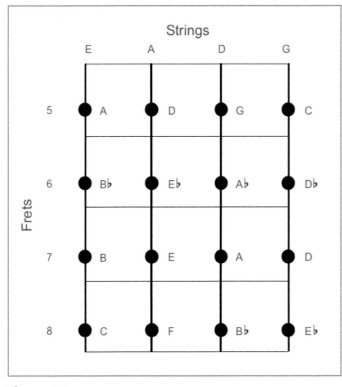

Figure 3.1
Note names: frets 5–8

Fifth Fret Trick

One thing to notice here is that the fifth fret on the E string is an A, which is the same pitch as the next open string. The same rule applies for the other strings. So if you're having trouble remembering the names of the notes on the fifth fret, just play the next open string, and there's your answer.

The last group of notes to memorize is located on frets 9 through 12 (see Figure 3.2). You're probably saying, "Yeah, but my bass has way more frets than 12." You're right, but the good news is that once you get up to the twelfth fret of the bass, the notes start over. The twelfth fret on the bass is the octave mark. That means that those notes are the same notes as your open strings—E, A, D, and G. Frets 13 through 16 are the same notes as frets 1 through 4. Frets 17 through 20 are the same notes as frets 5 through 8, and depending on how long your fretboard is, frets 21 through 24 are the same notes as frets 9 through 12.

Remember, you won't be able to memorize the note names overnight. I know it can seem overwhelming, but the trick is to focus on one group of notes at a time. Don't try to memorize the whole fretboard in one day, it's too much work. Work on them in groups of four notes at a time, one string at a time. Don't go on to frets 5 though 8 until frets 1 through 4 are finished. Pace yourself; it's really not bad, and the payoff will be huge in the end, I promise.

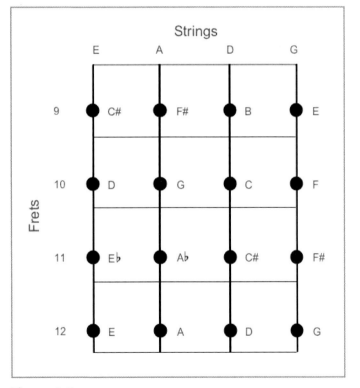

Figure 3.2
Note names: frets 9–12

Reading Music

NOW THAT YOU HAVE your note names memorized, let's check out a few basic things about reading music. Start with the *staff*. See Figure 3.3.

The Staff

A *staff* is a set of five horizontal lines. Notes are placed in different locations on the staff to indicate different pitches. A staff is read from left to right, just like a book. The height of a note determines its pitch. The higher a note is placed on the staff, the higher it will be in pitch. The lower a note is placed on the staff, the lower it will be in pitch.

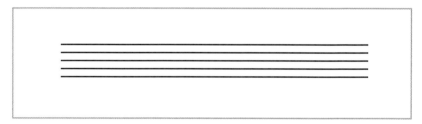

Figure 3.3
The staff

The Bass Clef

The *bass clef* is the symbol that sits all the way to the left of the staff and determines the pitch of written notes. Since you aspire to be a bass player, you'll be reading the bass clef.

Some other instruments that share the bass clef are the trombone, cello, and tuba. Even though you'll be reading bass clef, it's worth mentioning that the most popular clef used in music is called the *treble clef.* Notes written in treble clef are higher in pitch than notes written in bass clef. These notes are so high that you can't even play most of them on the bass. Figure 3.4 shows what the bass and treble clefs look like.

Bass Clef   Treble Clef

Figure 3.4
The bass and treble clefs

Time Signatures and Measures

A *time signature* relates to the timing of the music that you're reading. It tells you how many (top number) of a particular kind of note (bottom number) is in each measure. A *measure* indicates the notes or rests between two bar lines.

There are two numbers that make up a time signature. The top number tells you how many notes there are in each measure and the bottom number tells you what kind of notes there are. The most common time signatures are 4/4 (common time), 2/4 (cut time), and 3/4. So what exactly does that mean? Let's say you're in 4/4 time. The top number should be pretty clear. It's letting you know that there's four of a certain kind of note per measure. Now that bottom number will tell you the value of that note—it could be a 1, 2, 4, 8, or even 16.

Now you need to know the values of those bottom numbers. A number 1 on the bottom of a time signature equals a whole note. A number 2 equals a half note, a 4 equals a quarter note, an 8 equals an eighth note, and finally a 16 on the bottom equals a 16th note. So in 4/4 time, there are four quarter notes per measure. See Figure 3.5.

Figure 3.5
Time signature of 4/4 (four quarter notes in each measure)

If you have a time signature that says 2/4, that means that there are two quarter notes per measure. A 3/8 time signature means that there are three eighth notes per measure. A 5/16 time signature means that there are five 16th notes per measure.

Accidentals

What are those funny symbols next to some of the notes, you ask? They're called *accidentals*. An *accidental* is a notation symbol that is used to lower or raise the pitch of a note.

Sharps (♯)

Sharps raise the pitch of a note by one half step, or one fret.

Figure 3.6
A sharp accidental, showing D sharp in this case

Flats (♭)

Flats lower the pitch of a note by one half step, or one fret.

Figure 3.7
A flat accidental, showing D♭

In other words, the name of the note located on the third fret of the A string is called **C**. If I say to play a **C♯**, that means to play the note that is one fret higher than C, which would be located on the fourth fret, **C♯**. If I said to play a **C♭**, that would mean that you would play the note that is located one fret lower than a **C**, which would be on the second fret of the A string, **C♭**.

Key Signatures

A *key signature* is always placed right after the clef, and tells you the key of the music you're reading. The key signature will display the sharps or flats in the music in a particular order. Sharp order would be F♯, C♯, G♯, D♯, A♯, E♯, and B♯, and flats would be given in the order B♭, E♭, A♭, D♭, G♭, C♭, and F♭.

Figure 3.8
Order of sharps

When you see that a sharp or a flat is written in a specific space or line in a key signature, it means that every note that is played in that line or space will be sharp or flat. So if you see a B♭ in the key signature, all it means is that every time that you see a B written in the music you should actually play a B♭.

Figure 3.9
Order of flats

Notes on the Staff

O KAY, NOW THAT YOU have a general understanding of the basics, let's move on. I'm going to show you where the notes on the open strings of the bass are located on the staff. (An *open* string is when you play a string without pushing down a fret.) Let's look at them in order from lowest to highest—E, A, D, and G. See Figure 3.10.

Now that you can see where your open strings are located on the staff, you can fill in the gaps. The easiest way to remember the other notes on the staff is to break them down into lines and spaces. A *line* note means that the note sits on one of the five lines of the staff. A *space* note is a note that sits on one of the four spaces on the staff.

Figure 3.10
Open-string notes on the staff

Starting from the lowest line on the staff, our line notes will be G, B, D, F, and A. Our space notes, also from bottom to top, will be A, C, E, and G. See Figures 3.11 and 3.12.

Figure 3.11
Notes that sit on the lines

Let's take a few minutes and see where these notes are actually located on the bass. Start with the line notes. The G on the bottom line is located at the third fret of the E string. Remember, as the notes on the staff get higher, the pitches get higher as well. The second line, B, is located on the second fret of the A string. The third line, D, is your open D string. The fourth line, F, is played on the third fret of the D string, and the fifth line, A, is played on the second fret of the G string.

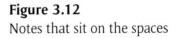

Figure 3.12
Notes that sit on the spaces

Think you've got it? What I want you to do is to play these notes one at a time. Start with G and work your way up. Once you find the note on the bass, I want you to actually say its name as you play it. Once you've done that, try playing the exercises shown in Figures 3.13 and 3.14. Go slowly and make sure to say the names of the notes as you play them.

Figure 3.13
Relating the line notes to the bass, exercise 3.1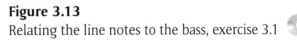

Figure 3.14
Relating the line notes to the bass, exercise 3.2

Now the space notes, also from bottom to top. A is your open A string. C, the second space, is the third fret on the A string. E is the second fret on the D string and G is the open G string. Just like before with the line notes, I want you to play each of these notes one at a time. When you find the note on the bass, say its name aloud. Now play the exercises shown in Figures 3.15 and 3.16.

Figure 3.15
Relating the space notes to the bass, 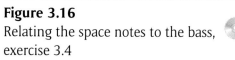 exercise 3.3

Figure 3.16
Relating the space notes to the bass, exercise 3.4

Figure 3.17 shows a diagram of all of the notes on the staff, with tablature included. Let's play these notes in order of pitch, regardless of whether they are placed on a line or a space. Start with the lowest line, G, and go all the way up to the highest line, A.

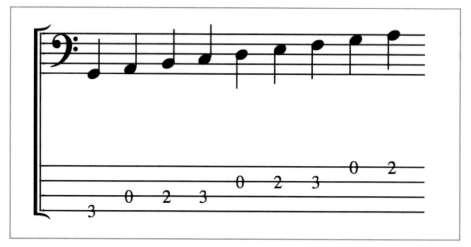

Figure 3.17
Notes on the staff with tablature

Right now I'm going to give you a master list of where all of
the notes on the first four frets of your bass are located on the
staff. See Figure 3.18. Use this as a reference if you find yourself
getting confused later on in the book.

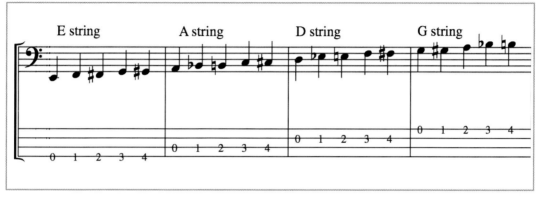

Figure 3.18
First four frets of the bass on the staff, with tablature

Ledger Lines

Why does the lowest note, E, have a line through it? That's called
a *ledger line*. Ledger lines are used to extend the staff. These are
used for notes that are really high or really low. See Figure 3.19.

Figure 3.19
Ledger lines

Okay, let's give it a shot. Right now I'm going to give you a few simple passages to read. All I want you to do is play the notes that you see on the staff. Don't worry about the rhythm yet, just focus on finding the notes on your bass. I include the tablature in Figures 3.20 and 3.21, but use it only to check yourself. Reading the tablature defeats the whole purpose of this exercise.

Figure 3.20
Exercise 3.5, reading music

Figure 3.21
Exercise 3.6, reading music

Those weren't so bad, right? Now I'll give you another couple passages (see Figures 3.22 and 3.23), but make sure you check the key signatures so that you know how many sharps or flats there are.

Figure 3.22
Exercise 3.7, reading music

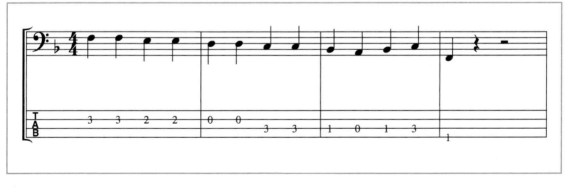

Figure 3.23
Exercise 3.8, reading music

Rhythm

N OW THAT YOU'VE LEARNED a bit about pitches, you're ready to take a look at the other element of reading music, rhythm. You know that placing a note in different places on the staff will determine its pitch, but now you need to know the duration of the note. How *long* do you play it?

Parts of a Note

There are three parts to a note: the note head, the stem, and the flag. All of these characteristics determine the value, or length, of a note. Figure 3.24 illustrates the parts of a note.

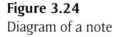

Figure 3.24
Diagram of a note

Note Values

Figure 3.25 shows a diagram of the most commonly used notes. Note that each line equals one whole note (two half notes equals one whole note, four quarter notes equals one whole note, and so on).

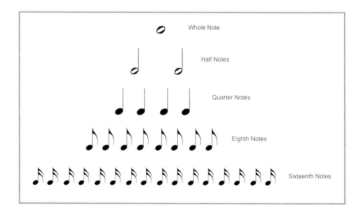

Figure 3.25
Triangle chart

Everything is based around the whole note. A note that lasts for half as long as a whole note is called a half note. A note that lasts for a quarter as long as a whole note is called a quarter note. This continues for all of the other notes as well (8th, 16th, and 32nd notes). You can think of these note relationships as fractions. Two half notes equal one whole note, four quarter notes equal one whole note, eight eighth notes equal one whole note, and so on. Now take a minute to actually feel the difference between how quarter notes and eighth notes sound. This would be a great time to take out your *metronome*. Turn the metronome on and set the BPM (beats per minute) to 70. You'll hear a bunch of clicks with some space in between them, right? What I want you to do is count to four with the clicks as they happen. On the first click say one, on the second click say two, on the third click say three, and on the fourth click say four. Repeat this a few times. What you're doing is counting the quarter notes.

Now that you feel comfortable with that, I'll show you what eighth notes sound like. Remember, eighth notes are twice as fast as quarter notes. All you have to do is add the word "and" in the spaces between the quarter notes. So you'll say "one and two and three and four and." The numbers are said with the clicks and the "ands" are said in the spaces between the clicks.

Practice going back and forth between quarter notes and eighth notes with your metronome. Try saying "1, 2, 3, 4," and then "1 and 2 and 3 and 4 and." Repeat this a bunch of times until it feels comfortable. Figure 3.26 shows a chart to show you what you're doing musically.

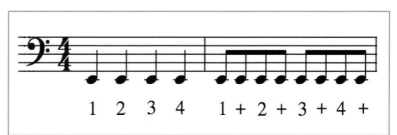

Figure 3.26
Quarter notes and eighth notes

It looks like a lot to take in, but it's actually pretty easy. Say you're in 4/4, or common time. The second, or bottom, number tells you what type of note makes up one beat of the measure. Since it's a 4 in this case, you know it's a quarter note. The first, or top, number tells you that there are four beats in each measure. So in 4/4 time, there are four quarter notes that make up one measure, as illustrated in Figure 3.27.

Figure 3.27
4/4 time means that four quarter notes make up the measure

In 3/4 time, three quarter notes make up one measure (see Figure 3.28).

Figure 3.28
Three quarter notes make up a measure in 3/4 time

Don't forget, there can also be variations on which notes make up the measure. For instance, in 4/4 you know that four quarter notes make up one measure, but there can also be any combination of other valued notes as long as you end up with the same value as four quarter notes per measure. In other words, there can be a 4/4 measure with eight eighth notes, as shown in Figure 3.29.

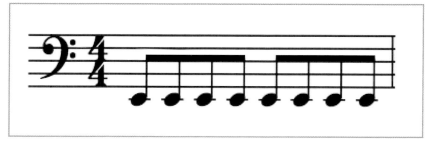

Figure 3.29
Eight eighth notes in a 4/4 measure

You can also have a 4/4 measure that has two quarter notes and four eighth notes, as shown in Figure 3.30.

Figure 3.30
Two quarter notes and four eighth notes in a 4/4 measure

You can also have a 4/4 measure with two half notes, as shown in Figure 3.31.

Figure 3.31
Two half notes in a 4/4 measure

There are many possibilities here. I'm going to write out a few examples for you to check out. See Figures 3.32 and 3.33.

Figure 3.32
Exercise 3.9, reading music: Melody from Arcade Fire's "Wake Up"

Figure 3.33
Exercise 3.10, reading music

The Dotted Note

If there is a little dot next to the note head, it is called a *dotted note.* This dot will change the value of the note. It simply adds one half of the note's value onto itself. For instance, a half note with a dot next to it adds a quarter note to its value. A quarter note with a dot next to it adds an eighth note to its value. See Figure 3.34.

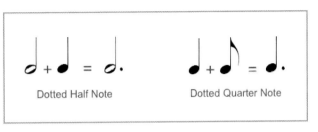

Figure 3.34
Dotted note values

So let's break down the dotted half note. A regular half note is two beats. One half of its original value is one beat. Two beats plus one beat equals three beats. A dotted half note gets three beats. Look for dotted notes in the examples at the end of the chapter.

Rests

Now on to rests. A *rest* is a moment of silence in music. It means that no sound is to be made for a certain amount of time. Just like note values, there are rest values as well. Figure 3.35 shows a chart of the different symbols for various rests.

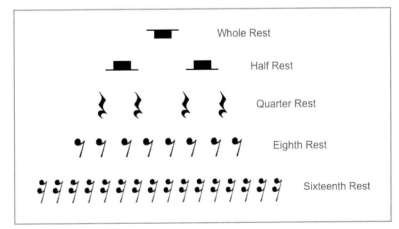

Figure 3.35
Rest chart

Note that there are whole note rests, half note rests, quarter note rests, eighth note rests, and even 16th and 32nd note rests. In terms of duration, rests work the same way as notes do. The only difference is that instead of playing a note for a certain amount of time, you are silent for that time. Figure 3.36 shows how those rests look on the staff.

Figure 3.36
Rests on the staff

Before You Start Playing

Before you move on to some more reading exercises, I want to point out a few things about reading music that helped me a lot.

Remember that there's a lot of stuff to look at before you start reading a musical passage. Before you play, you should look at the time signature and think about the timing of the song or piece. Is it in 4/4, 3/4, or 2/4? Then take a look at the key signature and determine the key of the piece. How many sharps or flats does the song have?

Counting

Counting while you read music is critical. I used to be a horrible reader, and I couldn't figure out why. It was because I wasn't counting through the beats of each measure; I was guessing. The right way to go about reading is to set up a *tempo*.

Tempo is Italian for *time*. A tempo refers to the pace or speed of a song or piece. Those numbers on your metronome refer to different tempos. Most metronomes range from about 40 to 200 beats per minute, which is slow to fast.

I like to give myself a count-off before I start. I turn on the metronome to an appropriate speed and count to four with the metronome and then start at the first measure. You should always have that metronome pulse going through your head. Feel free to count out loud if it helps you. Sometimes I even tap my foot to keep on track. When you get to a rest, you can actually say "rest" out loud.

Figure 3.37
Exercise 3.11, reading music

It's time to combine rests with written notes. Figures 3.37 and 3.38 are some basic examples of how rests might be used in written music. Take these exercises slowly and count. It's important to play these exercises the correct way. Slow and correct is much better than fast and sloppy. You'll move on to more advanced reading in later chapters.

Figure 3.38
Exercise 3.12, reading music

4

The Blues and
Major Scales in

Other Keys

IN MY OPINION, ALL MUSICIANS should have a
basic knowledge and understanding of the blues.
The reason being that the blues has influenced
almost all types of popular music, including rock and
roll, country, and jazz. As a bass player, I guarantee
that somewhere down the line you will be asked to
play a blues piece with someone. Because the tradi-
tional blues form is such a widely known language
among musicians, it can be a great thing to play with
someone whom you've never played with before.
Most musicians share the blues as a common language.
In addition to teaching you how to play the blues,
I'm going to show you an easy way to learn how to
play major scales in other keys.

A Little History

THE BLUES BECAME POPULAR in the United States in the early 1900s, but its roots go way back to Africa. African Americans took blues music with them when they were brought to this country in the early 20th century.

"The blues ... its 12-bar, bent-note melody is the anthem of a race, bonding itself together with cries of shared self-victimization. Bad luck and trouble are always present in the blues, and always the result of others, pressing upon unfortunate and down-trodden poor souls, yearning to be free from life's troubles. Relentless rhythms repeat the chants of sorrow, and the pity of a lost soul many times over. This is the blues."

—W.C. Handy (the "Father of the Blues")

Blues songs were generally written about suffering, hard times, and life's troubles. African laborers would sing these songs in groups while they were working. They were sung as chants, and for years they were recorded only by memory.

12-Bar Blues Form

The earliest blues music didn't necessarily have a standard measure or bar length until around the1930s, when the 12-bar blues became the standard. (*12-bar* refers to the amount of measures it takes to complete this blues pattern.) This blues form can be played in any key and only uses three chords. The chord chart is listed in Figure 4.1 in the key of G.

G	C or G	G	G
C	C	G	G
D	C	G	D or G

Figure 4.1
Blues form

Blues Bass Lines

So now you know what the chords are in a standard 12-bar blues, but what does the bass player play over these chords? The answer is that there are many possibilities. First, you'll start with some classic blues bass lines. I still play these bass lines. I promise that once you learn to play them, you too will find yourself using always these bass lines.

Remember that these blues lines can be played in any key. Once you understand what the blues form is, move to another key and try to play the same line. Try playing it in the keys of A and E, as shown in Figures 4.4 and 4.5.

These bass lines may sound really simple to you, and that's because they are. But the hard part isn't playing the right notes; it's playing them with the right feel. I'm talking about where you place the notes and how hard you feel the groove.

Figure 4.2
Blues bass line example 4.1 in G

Figure 4.3
Blues bass line example 4.2 in G

Figure 4.4
Blues bass line example 4.3 in A

The Blues Feel

If you hear a great blues band, you probably won't notice the bass player too much. A great blues bass player doesn't jump out and play a lot of notes; he or she lays back and plays simply, with a great feel. That's what's important about the blues—the feel.

Figure 4.5
Blues bass line example 4.4 in E

The Blues Scale

THERE ARE MANY OPINIONS on what the blues actually is. Some say it's a chord progression, a scale, or even a way of life. Basically, it means something different for everybody. However, there are some basic characteristics that are present in most blues music.

One main characteristic of blues music is the use of *blue notes.* Blue notes refers to the lowering of the third, fifth, and seventh degrees of a scale by a half step. Figure 4.6 shows a blues scale written out in the key of G.

Chances are that when you hear a blues solo, you'll hear tons of blue notes. The blues scale is used heavily in a lot of blues, jazz, and rock music. Get to know it well; it will become your friend.

Figure 4.6
The blues scale in G

Practicing the Blues Scale

There are tons of really fun ways to practice the blues scale. One obvious way is to just play the scale forward and then backward. Memorize the hand shape. You can easily play this scale without having to shift your hand. Figure 4.7 shows a great fingering example.

Fingering	1	4	1	2	3	1	3
String		E	E	A	A	A	D	D

Figure 4.7
Blues scale fingering

You can use this same fingering to play the blues scale in any key. Play this pattern starting on a different note. Try starting on an A, located on the fifth fret of the E string. Then try it starting on a B, located on the seventh fret of the E string. This hand shape, or fingering pattern, works regardless of which note you start on.

Once you have a pretty good grasp of the fingering, and more importantly the sound of the scale, try mixing up the order of the notes. Figure 4.8 shows one example.

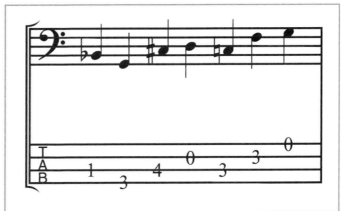

Figure 4.8
Mixed-up blues scale

Come up with your own order. You don't even have to play all of the notes in the scale every time. Maybe sometimes you'll only play three of the notes going up the scale, and five of the notes coming down. Feel free to mix up the rhythm as well. Take 10 minutes and just mess around with the blues scale. Play it however you want to. Figure out which notes sound the coolest to you and don't forget to try playing the scale in different keys.

Choose a different key each day and play the scale only in that key. So maybe Monday is the key of G, Tuesday is A, Wednesday is E, and so on. This will help you get familiar with the scale.

Try to come up with a pattern or riff that's based on the blues scale. Think of it as a section to a song. There are lots of blues-based riffs in music by artists such as Led Zeppelin, Rage Against the Machine, and Jimi Hendrix. Listen to these bands if you haven't already and check out the different ways they use the blues scale.

Learning Major Scales in Other Keys

L ET'S GO BACK to scale degrees. Remember that? That's when each note of the scale is assigned a number. You already learned about how to assign a number or scale degree to different notes in the scale. In a C major scale C is 1, D is 2, E is 3, F is 4, G is 5, A is 6, B is 7, and the top C is 8.

Here's a good trick to remember how to play a major scale. Memorize the fingering. If you can play one major scale, you can play them all just by starting on a different note.

For now, think of a major scale as going across three strings. Now remember the fingerings. On the first string all you have to remember is 2, 4, meaning middle finger and pinky. The second string is 1, 2, 4 or index, middle finger, and pinky. The third string is 1, 3, 4 or index, ring, pinky. The frets are irrelevant. No matter where you play that pattern, it's a major scale. Play that starting on a C for a C major scale. Start on an A for an A major scale, and so on.

Now the trick is to know how many sharps or flats are in the different major scales. The C major scale has no sharps and no flats.

The Circle of Fifths

I N MUSIC, YOU HAVE a total of 12 keys: C, G, D, A, E, B, F♯/G♭, C♯/D♭, A♭, E♭, B♭, and F. This pattern of notes is called the *circle of fifths.* Each of these keys has a different number of sharp or flat notes, and the circle of fifths is a really easy way of memorizing them.

Why is it called the *circle of fifths?* Because there are five notes between each key. Look at the first few keys: C, G, and D. If you start on C and go up five notes—C, D, E, F, G—you land on G, which is the second key in the circle. If you start on G and go up another five notes—G, A, B, C, D—you land on D, the third key in the circle. This pattern will go all the way around until you reach C again.

The circle of fifths can help you determine how many sharps or flats there are in a specific key or scale. The numbers inside the circle refer to the number of sharps or flats in that major scale. So for instance, the D major scale has two sharps, as shown in Figure 4.9.

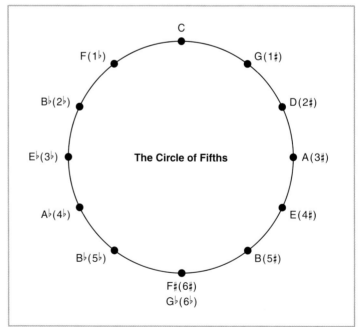

Figure 4.9
The circle of fifths

Now you're probably asking yourself, "How do I know which of the notes are sharp?" To get that answer, all you have to do is memorize this short list.

Sharps: F♯ C♯ G♯ D♯ A♯ E♯ B♯

This is the list of sharps, in order. So let's stay with the D major scale. The chart in Figure 4.9 says that it has two sharps, so based on the list they will be F♯ and C♯. Now if you play the major scale pattern that I showed you starting on a D, you'll see that the notes F♯ and C♯ are included in that scale.

There is a little trick that I'll let you in on. When you're in a sharp key, such as D, for example, you can find out which notes are sharp and how many sharps there are in that key or scale by finding D on the list of sharps and going back two letters. So, find D on the list. Go back two letters, so you're on C. Now C and whatever is before C are the sharp notes in that scale (C♯ and F♯). If you were in E major, you would go back two letter names to D, which means that there are four sharps in that key and they are F♯, C♯, G♯, and D♯.

That works for the sharps, but what about the flats? Luckily, the order of the flats is the same as the sharps, only backwards.

Flats: B♭ E♭ A♭ D♭ G♭ C♭ F♭

Here's a trick to remember the flats. Pick your key, let's say D♭. All you have to do is go up one more letter on the flat list, which would be G♭. Now you know that there are five flats in G♭, and they would be B♭, E♭, A♭, D♭, and G♭.

If you want to play an E♭ major scale, you would know that there are three flats, and that those flats are going to be B♭, E♭, and A♭.

The best way to fully grasp this is to put in the time and memorize the circle of fifths. Pick a key or a scale each week to focus on. You'll be surprised what 10 minutes a day can do for you. Practice them in order, starting with C major. All you need to do is play the scale, say the names of each of the notes as you play them, and take note of how many sharps or flats are in that scale or key. Major scales and key centers are two concepts that all musicians need to understand, and they don't take that long to memorize.

The Modes

A MODE IS A TYPE of scale. Just like a major or a minor scale, modes have seven different notes. There are seven modes in total and each mode has a different sound or tonal structure. This chapter shows you how each of the modes are constructed. Remember the first scale that you learned about, the C major scale? Let's start there.

Learning the Modes

THE FIRST THING THAT you're going to do is build a scale off of each note in a C major scale. All of the notes in each of the modes will be from the C major scale, so there won't be any sharps or flats. The first mode is called *Ionian,* and is illustrated in Figure 5.1.

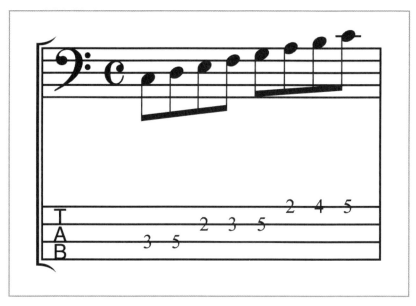

Figure 5.1
The Ionian mode is the C major scale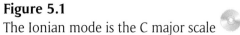

The *Ionian* mode is just the C major scale, plain and simple.

The second mode is called *Dorian,* and is illustrated in Figure 5.2. For this mode all you have to do is play a C major scale, but you start on a D and end on a D.

Figure 5.2
The Dorian mode

The third mode is called *Phrygian.* Same as before, you play a
C major scale. However, this time you start on an E and end on
an E. See Figure 5.3.

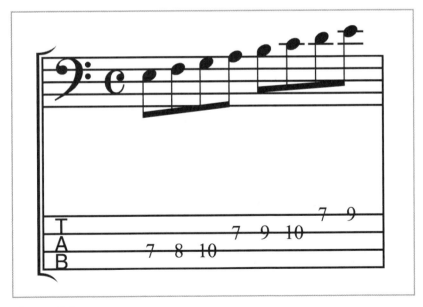

Figure 5.3
The Phrygian mode

See the pattern here? You're just playing the C major scale, but you start and end on different notes. Here are the names and notes of the last four modes:

- ▶ **Lydian (see Figure 5.4)**
- ▶ **Mixolydian (see Figure 5.5)**
- ▶ **Aeolian (see Figure 5.6)**
- ▶ **Locrian (see Figure 5.7)**

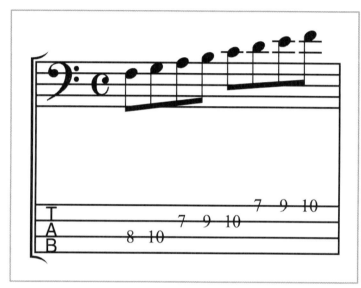

Figure 5.4
Lydian mode

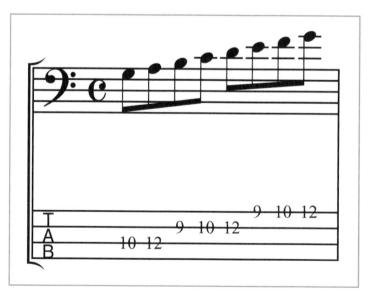

Figure 5.5
Mixolydian mode

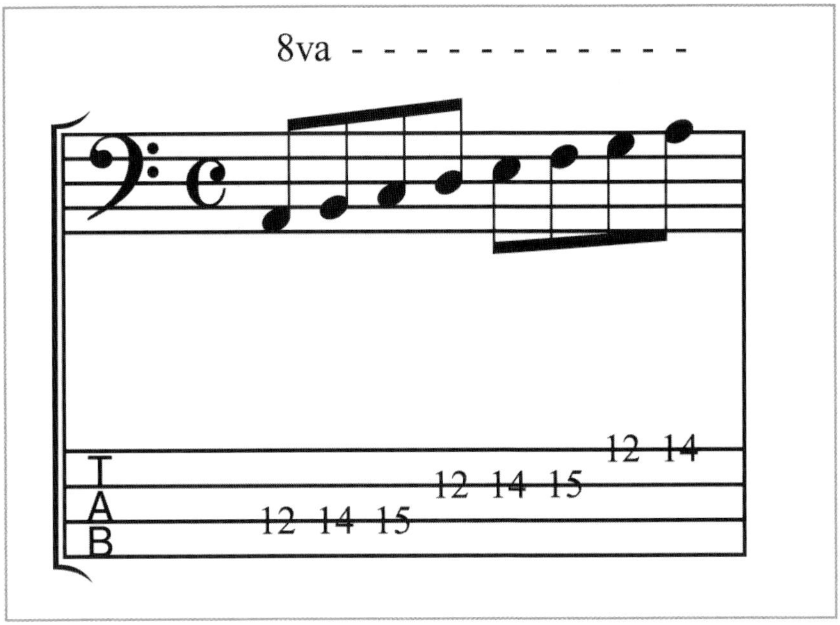

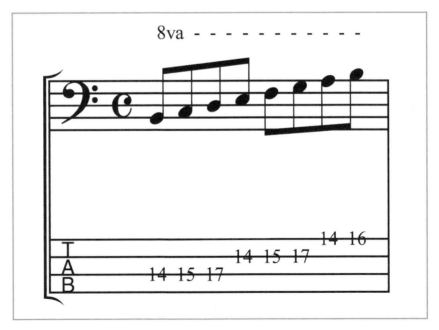

Figure 5.6
Aeolian mode

Figure 5.7
Locrian mode

Characteristics of the Modes

One easy way to memorize the modes is to break them down and note to yourself which scale degrees are characteristic to that mode. All flats and sharps are listed as changes to a major scale. This will help you when you are playing in keys other than C.

- ▶ Ionian—Major scale
- ▶ Dorian—♭3 and ♭7 (the third and seventh notes are lowered by a half step, or one fret)
- ▶ Phrygian—♭2, ♭3, ♭6, and ♭7 (the second, third, and seventh notes are lowered by a half step, or one fret)
- ▶ Lydian—♯4 (the fourth note is raised by a half step, or one fret)
- ▶ Mixolydian—♭7 (the seventh note is lowered by a half step, or one fret)
- ▶ Aeolian—♭3, ♭6, ♭7 (the third, sixth, and seventh notes are lowered by a half step, or one fret)
- ▶ Locrian—♭2, ♭3, ♭5, ♭6, ♭7 (the second, third, fifth, sixth, and seventh notes are lowered by a half step, or one fret)

Now let's look at some common fingerings for the modes on the electric bass. For this example, you'll start each mode on the A string. Each pattern is designed so that you do not have to shift. See Figures 5.8 through 5.14 for the proper fingering.

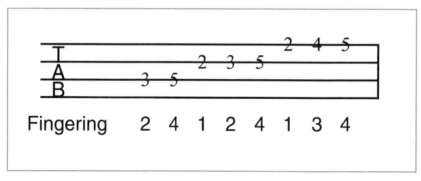

Figure 5.8
Ionian fingering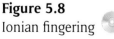

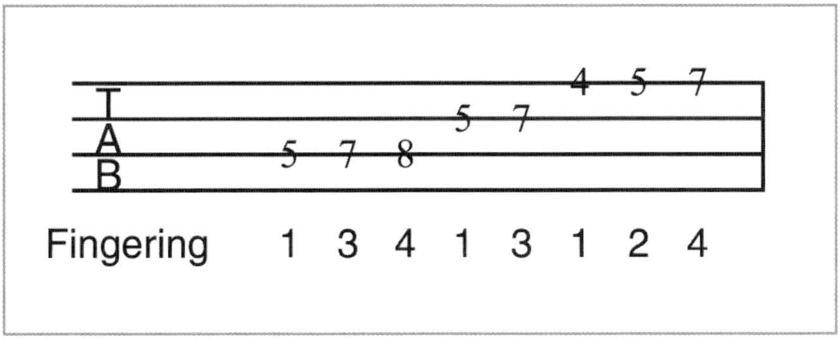

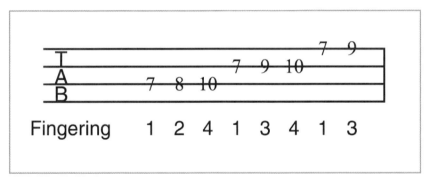

Figure 5.9
Dorian fingering

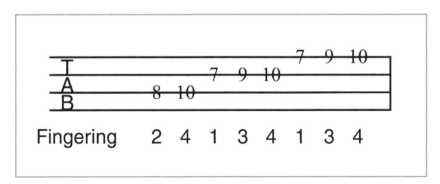

Figure 5.10
Phrygian fingering

Figure 5.11
Lydian fingering

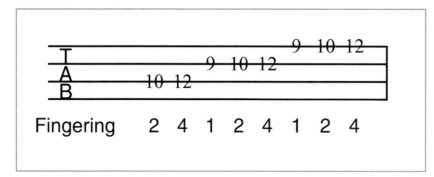

Figure 5.12
Mixolydian fingering

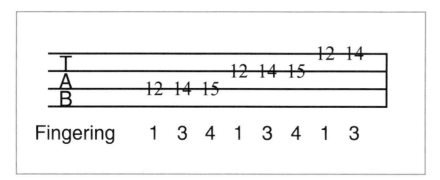

Figure 5.13
Aeolian fingering

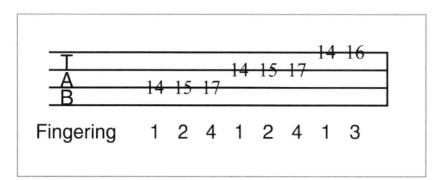

Figure 5.14
Locrian fingering

Practicing Modal Hand Shapes

Once you feel comfortable with the fingerings of the modal patterns, it's time to move on. A great thing to do is to mix up the order of the notes within a mode. First off, assign a number to each scale degree. For the Ionian mode in C major C=1, D=2, E=3, F=4, G=5, A=6, and B=7. Regardless of which mode you are playing, the first note will always be 1 and each note from there will go up in order. For example, in the Dorian mode D=1, E=2, F=3, and so on.

Now make up a series of numbers from 1–8 (8 will be the octave) and try plugging in the mode to fit your sequence. The sequences don't necessarily have to use all of the numbers. You can try them with just two or three numbers to start, and feel free to repeat notes. One example could be 1346. Figures 5.15 through 5.17 show some examples.

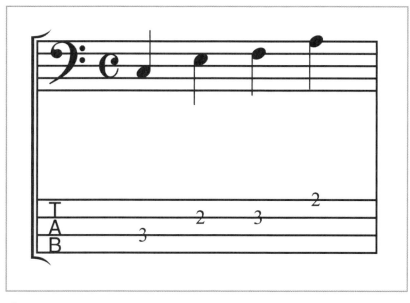

Figure 5.15
1346 Ionian

Try plugging in any set of numbers and take them through all of the modes. Try using your phone number or your birthday. Any set of numbers can help you practice modes!

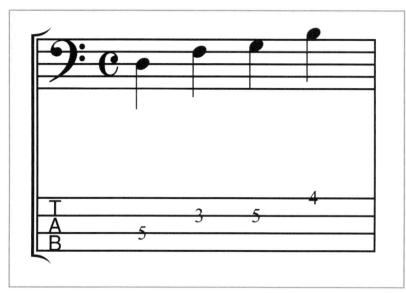

Figure 5.16
1346 Dorian

Figure 5.17
1346 Phrygian

Intervals and

Ear Training

THIS CHAPTER ADDRESSES a very important aspect of music: *ear training.* Being able to play your instrument will only get you so far. Being able to hear and identify what you or others are playing is equally, if not more, valuable. Ever hear a song on the radio and wish that you could figure out how to play it? Developing good ears will give you the tools to do just that. One cool thing about ear training is that you can work on it with a friend. I'll show you how. First you'll start with intervals.

Intervals

WHAT IS AN INTERVAL? It's basically the difference in pitch between two notes. Let's go back to the major scale for a minute. Remember when you learned about scale degrees? Each note in the scale can be given a number—C=1, D=2, E=3, F=4, and so on—as shown in Figure 6.1.

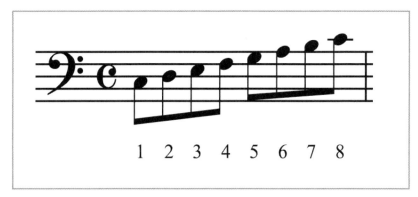

Figure 6.1
C major scale with assigned numbers

So say that you have two notes—C and D. The distance between those notes is called a major second. I'll explain. Think of it in terms of scale steps. D is the second note in a C major scale, therefore the difference between C and D is a major second. Further, the distance between C and E is a major third. When you're trying to determine the interval between two notes, count the number of scale steps between them, starting with 1 for the lowest note. If you have G and D for instance, the number of scale degrees between them is five (G, A, B, C, D), making the interval a fifth. Look at it on a staff, shown in Figure 6.2.

Figure 6.2
A perfect fifth

You're probably asking yourself what the point of all of this is, right? Well, it's not just knowing what the names of the intervals are, it's being able to hear and identify them. You want to train your ear to hear these intervals. So, the first step is being able to play them on your instrument. That brings you to the interval study.

Interval Study

FOR YOUR PURPOSES RIGHT now, you're going to deal with intervals starting with unison and ending with an octave. I'll explain. First, this is all based off of the C major scale.

Let's check it out. Figures 6.3 through 6.10 list all of the intervals within a C major scale:

- ▶ Unison, C to C (see Figure 6.3)

- ▶ Major second, C to D (see Figure 6.4)

- ▶ Major third, C to E (see Figure 6.5)

- ▶ Perfect fourth, C to F (see Figure 6.6)

- ▶ Perfect fifth, C to G (see Figure 6.7)

- ▶ Major sixth, C to A (see Figure 6.8)

- ▶ Major seventh, C to B (see Figure 6.9)

- ▶ Octave, C to C (see Figure 6.10)

Figure 6.3
Unison, C to C

Figure 6.4
Major second, C to D

Figure 6.5
Major third, C to E

Figure 6.6
Perfect fourth, C to F

Figure 6.7
Perfect fifth, C to G

Figure 6.8
Major sixth, C to A

Figure 6.9
Major seventh, C to B

Figure 6.10
Octave, C to C

Where Are These Intervals on the Bass?

So now you have to figure out how you're going to play these intervals. Where are they located? I'll help.

The first interval is unison, meaning the same note is played twice. All you have to do is play the same note, C, twice. Now you can play that C on the third fret of the A string two times in a row, or you can play the first C on the eighth fret of the E string and the second one on the third fret of the A string, or any combination of those. Figure 6.11 shows what it looks like in tablature.

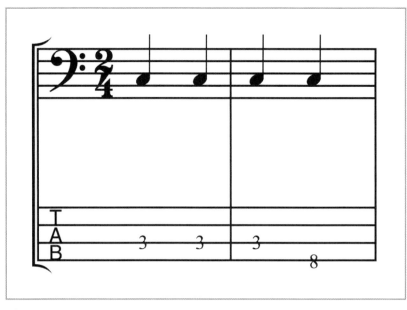

Figure 6.11
Tablature of unison

The next interval is a major second, C to D. There are a few ways to play this interval on the bass. Let's look at the options. See Figure 6.12.

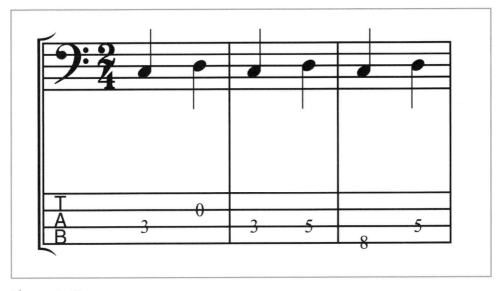

Figure 6.12
Tablature: A major second

Notice that even though you're using different fingerings, the set of notes will still sound the same. C to D sounds like C to D no matter where you play it, and that goes for the rest of the intervals too.

Figures 6.13 through 6.18 show the other six intervals from the major scale:

> ► **A major third (see Figure 6.13)**

> ► **A perfect fourth (see Figure 6.14)**

> ► **A perfect fifth (see Figure 6.15)**

> ► **A major sixth (see Figure 6.16)**

> ► **A major seventh (see Figure 6.17)**

> ► **An octave (see Figure 6.18)**

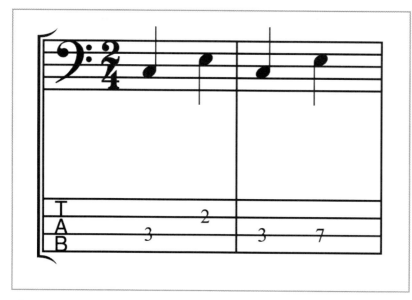

Figure 6.13
Tablature: A major third

Figure 6.14
Tablature: A perfect fourth

Figure 6.15
Tablature: A perfect fifth

Figure 6.16
Tablature: A major sixth

Figure 6.17
Tablature: A major seventh

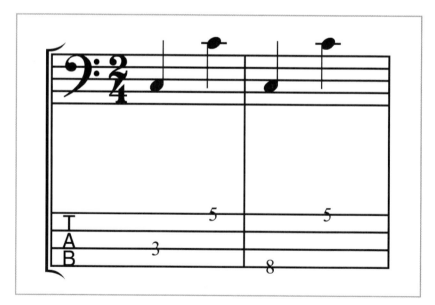

Figure 6.18
Tablature: An octave

Now that you have all of the information, it's important to spend some time with each interval. This doesn't take long at all. All that I want you to do is play through all of the possibilities. Spend a few minutes on each one. Start with unison and slowly make your way up to the octave. It's important to think about the sound and the distance in pitch between each interval. A great way to get to know the sound of an interval is to play both notes and then sing them. You can sing quietly; no one has to hear you.

Interval Hand Shapes

A great way of memorizing intervals is to think about the hand shapes that you're creating. I want you to take notice of what your hand looks like as you're playing these intervals. What will happen is that you will start to associate different fingerings with each interval. For instance, I know that when I play a major third, my fingering hand will make the shape shown in Figure 6.19.

In my head, I'm saying, "Okay, a major third. I'll play a C with my second finger (on the third fret of the A string), and if I go up one string (the D string) and back one fret, I'll have the shape of a major third."

I promise that this hand shape association idea will make playing intervals second nature for you. All you have to do is pay attention to what your hands are doing. Easy enough, right?

When you feel like you're getting comfortable with playing these intervals, you can start practicing with a friend. Here's how.

Figure 6.19
A major third

Practicing Intervals with a Friend

THIS IS A FUN WAY TO LEARN how to identify intervals. I used to do this with my best friend in high school who was a guitar player. All you need is a friend who plays an instrument. Here's what you do. First, sit back to back with your friend, so that you can't see each other's hands. Have one person play an interval on their instrument and have the other person try to play it back on their own instrument. For right now you should always start on the note C. Sound easy? Try it. Feel free to play the interval a few times to help the other person figure it out.

I guarantee that if you dedicate just a few minutes out of each day to this exercise, your ears will develop very quickly. This is the first step in being able to play your favorite songs!

Specialty

Techniques

THE ELECTRIC BASS IS AN instrument with endless sonic possibilities. Plucking the strings with your index and middle fingers is probably the most common way to get sound out of the instrument, but there are so many other options. What would the instrument sound like if you plucked the strings with your thumb? Or what if you hit the strings with the palm of your hand? Ever think about using your plucking hand to press down notes on the fingerboard? This chapter covers a few specialty bass techniques like slapping and tapping.

Slap Bass

*S*LAP BASS IS A PERCUSSIVE technique that consists of two actions: using the side of your thumb to hit the strings of the bass (slapping) and snapping the strings with your middle or index finger (popping). Both are done with your plucking hand. This was the first alternate sound technique that I learned on the electric bass. When I think about slap bass, I imagine a drum set. I think of slaps as bass drum hits and pops as a snare drum hits. This style of playing was developed, and for the most part introduced, by a bass player named Larry Graham. Slapping is most common in funk and pop music. Let's start.

Slapping

The slap is a crucial element of the slap bass technique. What you're trying to do is slap the string close to the fretboard with the side of your thumb. A common problem for beginners is getting a good amount of sound from the string. The key here is to hit the string and quickly move your thumb away. The best way to practice this is by repetition. Try hitting the low E string with your thumb. Are you getting the note to ring or does it sound dead?

There are a few things to keep in mind when trying to get a good sound out of a slap, and they all have to do with your plucking hand. The first thing is the angle of your hand. What I want you to do is make a fist and stick your thumb out.

Figure 7.1
Slap fist

Now line up your hand with the bass. Make sure that your thumb is parallel to the strings.

Another thing to be aware of is the part of the thumb that will be hitting the strings. If you take a look at your thumb, you will notice a bone that is located below your nail. It's about halfway down your thumb, right where your finger bends. That is the ideal spot for getting a clear slap sound out of your bass.

Figure 7.2
Lining up with the strings

Now I'll give you an exercise to practice what you just learned. You're going to slap each of the open strings four times. All I want you to concentrate on is getting a clean sound out of each note. Use your fingering hand to mute the strings that are not being played. As usual, go slowly and repeat the exercise until you have a handle on it.

Once you feel like you're getting a good slap sound, you can move on to the other part of slap bass, popping.

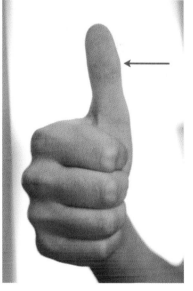

Figure 7.3
Slap contact point

Figure 7.4
Open-string slap exercise

Popping

Popping is simple and is usually done on the D and G strings. All you need to do is get your index or middle finger under the string and give it a slight pull, so that it makes a snapping sound. For now, try it with your index finger and make sure not to pull too hard; you don't want to break the string.

Here's a basic exercise that will help you learn to combine slapping and popping.

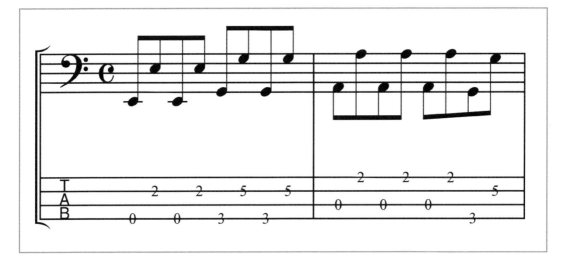

Figure 7.5
Combining slapping and popping

Hammering

The next step in the slap bass process is the hammer-on. Also known as "hammering," this technique will bring your slapping to a whole new level, and it's easy. What I want you to do is slap the open E string and once it starts ringing, push down on the second fret with your fingering hand. So you're slapping the string once, and getting two notes to sound, one right after the other.

Try this a few times. The little curve written below the two notes indicates that you only need to strike the first note, and the other note or notes are being "hammered" on. One attack, two notes, as shown in Figure 7.6.

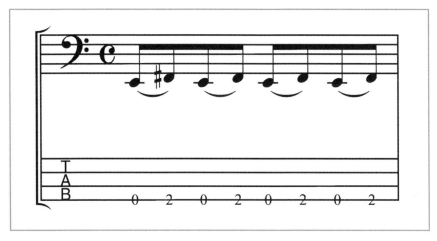

Figure 7.6
Hammering exercise

You can also hammer-on when you're popping. Pop a note and then press down another note with your fingering hand. Figure 7.7 shows an example.

Figure 7.7
Hammering exercise, with pop

Now let's combine the two techniques with hammer-ons (see Figure 7.8). Focus on the sound and the coordination between your fingering and plucking hands. Slap bass is all muscle memory in the beginning. If you spend just a few minutes a day on this technique, your hands will start to remember the patterns and you won't have to focus as hard.

Figure 7.8
Slapping and popping

For these next two examples (see Figures 7.9 and 7.10) I'm going to specify exactly how I want you to attack these notes:

▶ **A letter "T" indicates that the note is to be slapped with your thumb.**

▶ **A letter "P" indicates a pop with your index or middle finger.**

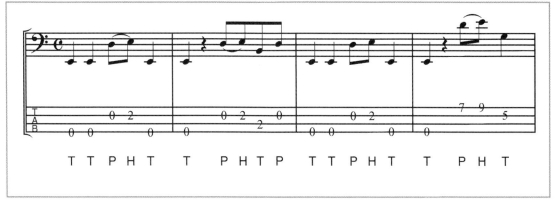

Figure 7.9
Slapping and popping

Figure 7.10
Slapping and popping

Thumb, Hammer, Pluck

This technique was developed by Victor Wooten. The basic idea is that you slap a note with the thumb of your plucking hand, hammer a note with your fingering hand, and pop or "pluck" a note with your plucking hand. Once you learn the coordination, you can apply any notes that you like. Figure 7.11 shows a basic example. The letter "H" indicates that the note is to be hammered.

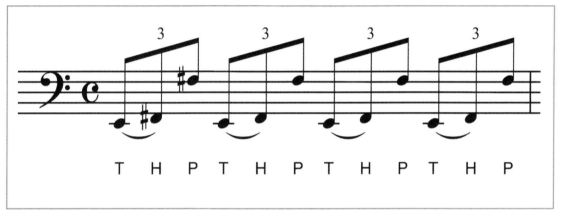

Figure 7.11
Thumb, hammer, and pluck

Figure 7.12 shows a thumb, hammer, pluck exercise to check out when you start to feel comfortable with the technique. Furthermore, if you'd like to hear some amazing bass players that use slap technique, check out Les Claypool ("Tommy the Cat" from the album *Sailing the Seas of Cheese*), Victor Wooten ("Classical Thump" from the album *A Show of Hands*), Larry Graham ("Pow" from the album *My Radio Sure Sounds Good to Me*), and Marcus Miller (his version of "Teen Town" from the album *The Sun Don't Lie*). You will not be disappointed.

Chapter 7

Figure 7.12
Thumb, hammer, pluck technique, advanced example

Triplets

Now would also be a good time to talk about the little number 3 that's written above the groups of notes in Figure 7.11. Those groups of 3s are called triplets. Remember from Chapter 3 what a note value is? Recall that two quarter notes equal one half note, and four eighth notes equal two quarter notes. Well, consider what happens when you want to fit three notes into the space of two. You get what's called a *triplet*. In Figure 7.11, the number 3 indicates that three eighth-note triplets are to be played evenly over the space of two eighth notes.

Tapping

TAPPING IS A TECHNIQUE where you tap the strings against the fretboard to get a sound. This can be done with both your fingering hand and your plucking hand. It's as if you're treating your bass like a piano. You don't need to pluck the note with one hand and finger it with the other; you're doing both with the same hand. I'll show you. What I want you to do is take the index finger of your fingering hand and press down on the 10th fret of the A string, just as if you were going to play a note on a piano. Do not use your plucking hand at all. The goal is to get a clean sound out of the note without having to pluck it. Try it a few times; it takes a little getting used to.

I want you to be aware of a few things while working on this. The first is that you want to avoid string noise or buzzing. If you are not plugged into an amplifier, this will be nearly impossible. Another thing to focus on is the end of the note, or the cut-off. You don't need to lift your finger completely off of the string to make the note stop. Lifting it just a little bit will get the job done.

Once you feel like you can get a nice sound out of the note by using your fingering hand, I want you to try the same thing with your plucking hand. That's right, take the index finger of your plucking hand and try getting a sound out of that same note, the 10th fret on the A string. Just like with your fingering hand, try to avoid buzzing and be aware of the sound of the note when you cut it off.

Honestly, this should take some practice. This isn't a technique that you will master overnight—if it were easy, everyone would do it. Once you feel like you can get a clean, focused sound from each hand, I want you to move on to the next exercise (see Figure 7.13) where you'll combine the two.

This will be simple. I'm going to give you two notes to play, one with each hand. Your fingering hand will play a G on the 10th fret of the A string and your plucking hand will play a D on the 12th fret of the D string. Use your index fingers for both. All that I want you to do is alternate between these two notes.

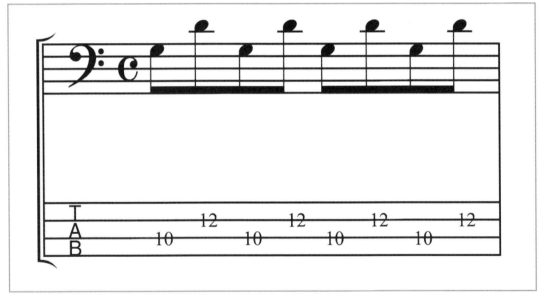

Figure 7.13
Tapping with two hands, two fingers

Again, just like with slapping, this is all muscle memory. Practice slowly and this will all start to feel like second nature to you. Once this feels comfortable, I want you to move on to the next exercise in Figure 7.14. All we're doing here is adding another note that will be played with the ring finger of your plucking hand.

Figure 7.14
Tapping with two hands, three fingers

Just to review: The G on the 10th fret of the A string should be played with the index finger of your fingering hand, the D on the 12th fret of the D string should be played with the index finger of your plucking hand, and the A on the 14th fret of the G string should be played with the ring finger of your plucking hand.

Now that you can do that, try tapping a C major scale. I want you to use the same fingering that I showed you in Chapter 2, except every time that you play a note on the fifth fret, I want you to use either the index or middle finger of your plucking hand. Whichever finger feels more natural is fine.

Figure 7.15
Tapping through a C Major scale

Now you should try to go up and down the scale, and if you really want to get good at it try tapping through all of the modes.

Tapping with Harmonics

So up to this point you've learned the basic idea of tapping on the electric bass. Now I'm going to show you a cool variation on that. What I want you to do is take the middle finger of your plucking hand and lightly tap on the 12th fret of the G string. Instead of tapping in the middle of the fret I want you to tap on the string right over the actual fret bar. After you pluck the note, take your finger off of the fret. This note should ring for a while and will have a "bell-like" tone. That's called a *harmonic.* Now try it on the 12th fret of any string. They should all work.

Once you have that figured out, it's time to move on to an easy two-hand harmonic tapping exercise. The notes tapped with your fingering hand will just be normal notes. The notes tapped with your plucking hand will be harmonics on the 12th fret.

For now, every time that you play the G harmonic I want you to use your middle finger, and every time that you play the D harmonic you should use your index finger. A circle over the note indicates that it's a harmonic.

Feel free to change the note that you're playing with your fingering hand; it doesn't have to stay on G. Move it around and find some other combinations that you like. You can also try changing the order of the harmonics. Come up with your own exercise.

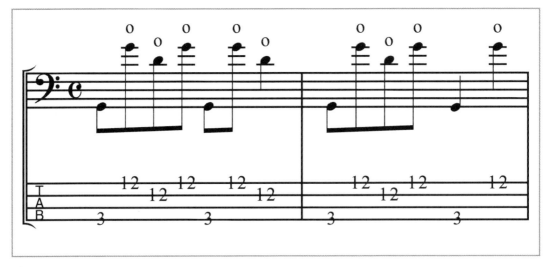

Figure 7.16
Tapping with harmonics

False Harmonics

Just to take this one step further, I'd like to show you another cool thing with harmonics. This is called the *false harmonic.* You just learned that if you tap on the 12th fret of any open string, you will hear the open harmonic. That note sounds as one octave above the open string. That's great if you want to play the notes E, A, D, or G, but what if you want to play a B flat or a C sharp? That's where the false harmonic comes in. Just to review, tap the 12th fret of the G string so that you get a clear harmonic sound. It should sound almost like a bell. Now what I want you to do is to push down on the first fret of the G string. Hold that note down and tap on the 13th fret of the G string. Hear it? That sound is one octave higher than the fret that you're fingering. It's a false harmonic. This will work with any note on the bass. The rule is that you tap on the fret that is 12 frets above the note that you are fingering. For instance, if you were fingering the note C located on the third fret of the A string, the false harmonic would be located on the 15th fret of the A string. You just add 12 to the fret number that you're fingering.

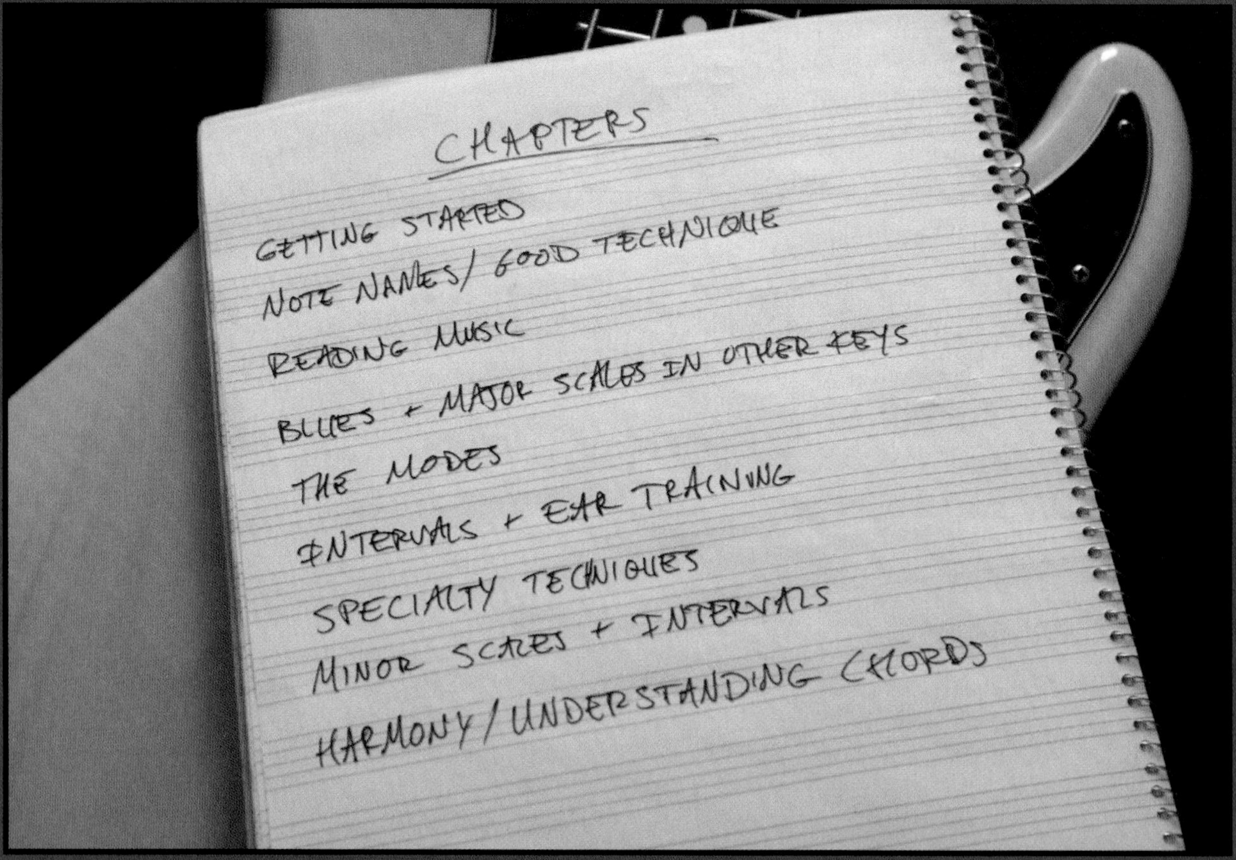

CHAPTERS

GETTING STARTED

NOTE NAMES / GOOD TECHNIQUE

READING MUSIC

BLUES + MAJOR SCALES IN OTHER KEYS

THE MODES

INTERVALS + EAR TRAINING

SPECIALTY TECHNIQUES

MINOR SCALES + INTERVALS

HARMONY / UNDERSTANDING CHORDS

Minor Scales

and Intervals

U P UNTIL THIS POINT in the book, I've been basing almost all of the theory around a C major scale. Now that you have a handle on that scale, it's time to move on to the minor scales. Believe it or not, you already know how to play a minor scale. Remember when you read about *modes* in Chapter 5? The Aeolian mode, which was discussed in that chapter, is a natural minor scale. See Figure 8.1.

Figure 8.1
Aeolian or A natural minor scale

How Major and Minor Scales Differ

PLAY THROUGH THAT SCALE with the same fingering that you used in Chapter 5. You'll notice that whereas major scales sound happy and almost cheerful, minor scales have a sad quality. Figure 8.2 shows a C major scale next to a C minor scale. Play them both, one right after the other, and listen for that change in quality.

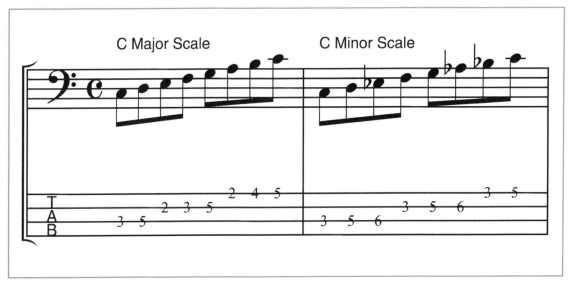

Figure 8.2
C major scale followed by a C minor scale

Which notes change? The third, sixth, and seventh notes are lowered, giving you E♭, A♭, and B♭. So if you know how to play a major scale, you can play a minor scale. You just lower the third, sixth, and seventh notes by a half step. Now I want you to take a minute and try to play a D minor scale. Then move on and play a G minor scale. Don't look at the music yet. Once you think you've got it figured out, you can check yourself against Figures 8.3 and 8.4.

Figure 8.3
D minor scale

Figure 8.4
G minor scale

Why do major and minor scales sound different? They are different because they're made up of different intervals, or series of whole and half steps. Remember that a major scale follows the following pattern: whole step, whole step, half step, whole step, whole step, whole step, half step. See Figure 8.5.

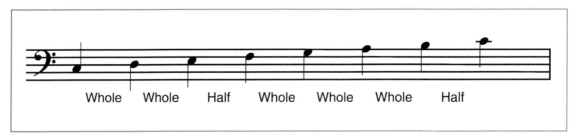

Figure 8.5
Intervals for a C major scale

A minor scale is made up of a different combination: whole, half, whole, whole, half, whole, whole. See Figure 8.6.

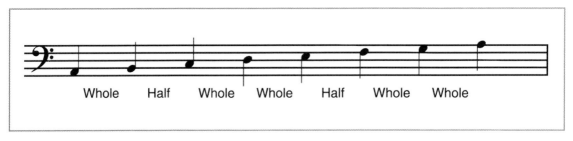

Figure 8.6
Intervals for an A minor scale

Review: Fingerings

IN THE BEGINNING I think it's a good idea to start minor scales with the index finger of your fingering hand, as shown in Figure 8.7. It's also a good idea to play major scales starting with the middle finger of your fingering hand, as shown in Figure 8.8. You then don't have to shift when you play the scales.

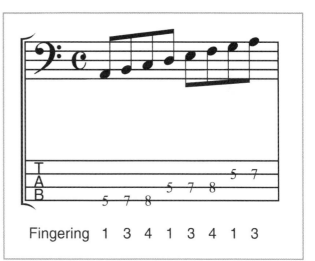

Figure 8.7
Minor scale fingering

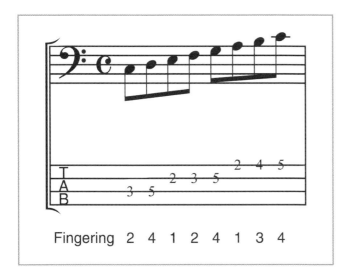

Figure 8.8
Major scale fingering

Relative Minor

CHAPTER 4 COVERED the major key signatures in the circle of fifths. Well, just like major keys, there are minor keys as well. Figure 8.9 shows a new circle of fifths chart that includes the minor keys.

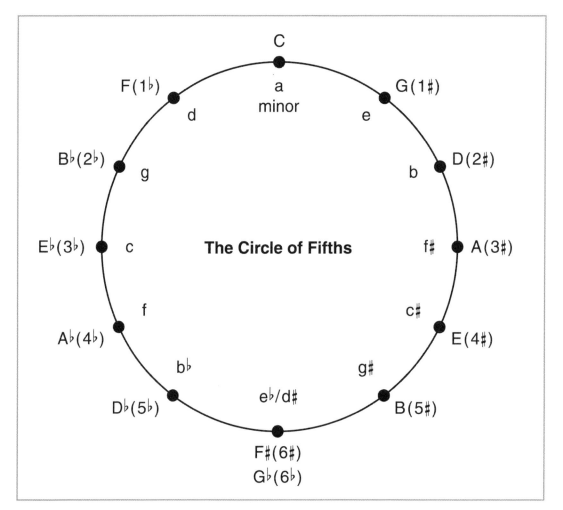

Figure 8.9
The circle of fifths with minor keys

Figuring out a key's relative minor is easier than you think. For instance, based on the new circle of fifths chart in Figure 8.9, you see that C major and A minor both have no sharps and no flats. They have the same number of accidentals, which is none. I like to think of the two as sharing the same scale, just starting in a different place. If you take a major scale and go down three half steps from the first note, the note that you land on is the relative minor key. So if you are in C major, you go down three half steps from C (B, B♭, A), which gives you A minor. C major and A minor share the same key signature. Now, what is the relative minor of A major? Go down three half steps from the root note A (A♭, G, F♯), which gives you F♯. A major and F♯ minor share the same key signature. Check it on the circle of fifths chart in Figure 8.9.

A Major (3 Sharps)

F♯ Minor (3 Sharps)

Figure 8.10
The relative minor of A major is F♯ minor

Minor Interval Study

IN CHAPTER 6, YOU READ about the importance of intervals and ear training. Let's take a moment to explore the different ways to play the remaining minor intervals. Even though these fingerings apply to all keys, the examples here use A minor.

The minor third is shown in Figure 8.11.

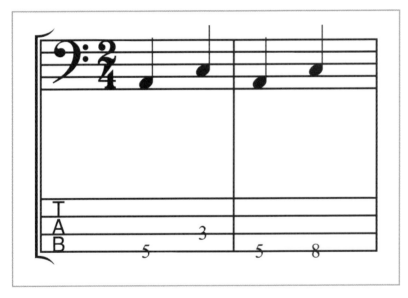

Figure 8.11
Fingerings for a minor third, A to C

The minor sixth is shown in Figure 8.12.

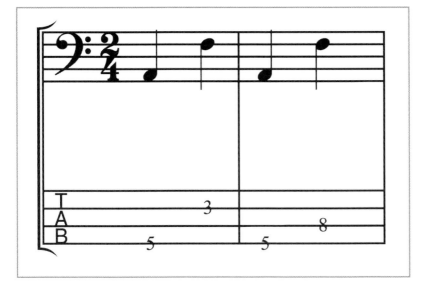

Figure 8.12
Fingerings for a minor sixth, A to F

The minor seventh is shown in Figure 8.13.

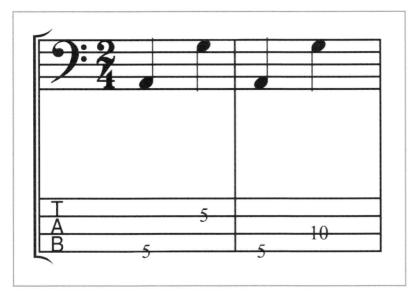

Figure 8.13
Fingerings for a minor seventh, A to G

Remaining Intervals

NOW THAT YOU'VE COMPLETED the minor interval study, I'll show you the only two remaining intervals within the octave. These intervals are not present in the major or the minor scale. They are called the minor second (or flat 2) and the *tritone*. The minor second interval is easy; it's just a half step. So, in the key of C, the minor second is D♭. See Figure 8.14.

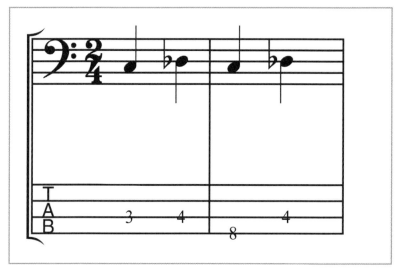

Figure 8.14
A minor second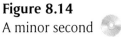

The last interval is an important one; it's called the tritone. This interval used to be called "the devil in music" for its evil-sounding quality. This goes back to the 18th century when members of the Church would be punished for singing a tritone. The tritone consists of three whole steps. In the key of C, the tritone would be F♯. Figure 8.15 shows this tritone.

You now know how to play every interval within the octave. It's really important to familiarize yourself with the sounds of these intervals. If there's one thing that I wish I had worked on more when I was starting out as a bass player, this would be it. So now when you work on intervals, either by yourself or with a friend, add the minor second and the tritone to the list.

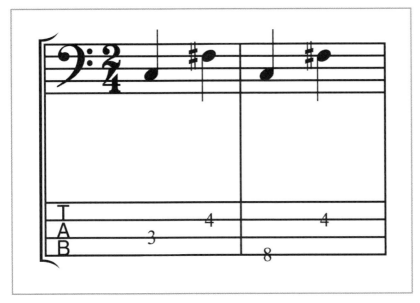

Figure 8.15
The tritone, sometimes called "the devil in music"

How Do You Practice Intervals?

QUIZZING YOURSELF WITH a friend who plays an instrument is a really fun way to work on this. You play an interval and the other person can either guess the name of the interval or try to play it back to you. Obviously, it would be hard to set that up regularly, so you should have a way of practicing by yourself too. What I do is pretty simple. I sit down with my bass and just work on one type of interval at a time. First I pick an interval; let's say I want to practice sixths. Next, I pick a key. Let's say C major. Then I play the root notes of the scale (C, D, E, F, G, A, B, and C) followed by a sixth above each note. If you stay in the key of C (no sharps and no flats), this will give you a mixture of major and minor sixths.

Once I feel comfortable playing that interval, I mix up the order of the scale. I just make things up that sound good to me. That's also a way to come up with ideas for songs. Just explore and play around with one interval at a time. You can easily spend an entire day practicing one type of interval. If you feel like you've really got a handle on that specific interval in one key, switch to a different key and try the same thing. Think about it—if you dedicate only 10 minutes a day to working on this, you'll get through every interval in no time.

Root	Sixth	
C	A	Major Sixth
D	B	Major Sixth
E	C	Minor Sixth
F	D	Major Sixth
G	E	Major Sixth
A	F	Minor Sixth
B	G	Minor Sixth
C	A	Major Sixth

Harmonic and Melodic Minor Scales

HE MINOR SCALE THAT you just learned is called a *Natural Minor scale.* It is one of three minor scales. The other two are called *Harmonic Minor* and *Melodic Minor.* The differences between the three are very subtle and deal only with the sixth and seventh notes of the scale.

Harmonic Minor Scale

The Harmonic Minor scale is just like the Natural Minor scale, which you should already know how to play. All you need to do to make it Harmonic Minor is raise the seventh note of the scale a half step. In the key of A minor, a Harmonic Minor scale looks like Figure 8.16.

Figure 8.16
The Harmonic Minor scale

Melodic Minor Scale

Once you have a good foundation, the Melodic Minor scale is easy too. Take your Natural Minor scale and raise the sixth and seventh notes a half step. So basically, you're playing a Natural Minor scale with a major sixth and major seventh, as shown in Figure 8.17.

Figure 8.17
The Melodic Minor scale

The best way to get a grasp on these scales is to play them over and over and really listen to the way that they sound. Add these scales to your ear training practice. You already know how to practice intervals with a friend, so you can now add scales. Play major, Natural minor, Harmonic minor, and Melodic minor scales to each other and see if you can figure out which ones are which. I promise that you will thank yourself down the road for learning these scales early on.

Harmony: Playing
and Understanding

Chords

THE PURPOSE OF THIS CHAPTER is to give you an introduction to *harmony*. Now that you're a bass player, I can promise you that other musicians, especially guitarists and piano players, will constantly be showing you the chords to different songs. The best way for you to understand what they're talking about is to know a little bit about chords yourself. By the end of this chapter, you're going to know what different chords sound like, which chords go together, and even how to play a few chords on the bass. Let's start.

What Is a Chord?

A CHORD IS WHEN THREE or more notes are played at the same time. Take a look at a C major chord, shown in Figure 9.1.

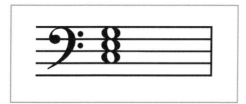

Figure 9.1
A C major chord

You remember the C major scale. A C major chord is when you play the first, third, and fifth note of the scale, C, E, and G, at the same time. Now a series of chords played in a row is called a *chord progression.* All of your favorite songs, whether the style is rock, jazz, funk, classical, or pop, follow some sort of chord progression. Let's look at another chord in the key of C, F major. Remember, when you're in C major you keep the key signature of C major. No sharps, no flats. See Figure 9.2.

Figure 9.2
An F major chord

Now how did I know which notes make up an F major chord? I played the first, third, and fifth notes of the C major scale, but starting on the note F this time. That gives me the notes F, A, and C. In relation to the C major scale, the note F is the fourth note, or scale degree, right? (C, D, E, F). So you can call that F chord the "four" chord. Chords are usually displayed in roman numerals, so four would be displayed as IV. In C major, the C chord is the I (pronounced "one") chord, and the F chord is the IV (pronounced "four") chord. Now take a look at another chord, G major, also known as the V (pronounced "five") chord.

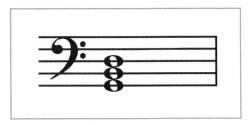

Figure 9.3
A G major chord

Again, this chord consists of three notes, the first, third, and fifth notes of the C major scale, but starting on the note G. That gives you G, B, and D. This is the V chord in C major. Have you noticed anything in terms of intervals with these major chords? Go back and play the chords, one note at a time. C, E, G then F, A, C, followed by G, B, D. Besides being able to play them all with the same fingering, they're all made up of the same intervals—a major third followed by a minor third. Start with the I chord, C major. The distance between the first two notes (C and E) is a major third and the distance between the second two notes (E and G) is a minor third.

What Do These Chords Sound Like?

B ASS PLAYERS ARE RARELY ASKED to play chords. We're usually asked to play the bottom, or *root note,* of a chord. That's fine, but how are you supposed to know what different chords sound like? This next exercise will help you to hear the differences between major and minor chords. Playing three notes at the same time can sound muddy on a bass; however, you can get a very nice sound out of playing two notes at once, also known as a *double stop,* on the bass as long as the intervals are far enough apart. The next section explains double stops in more detail.

Major Double Stops

Let's start with a C major chord. You now know that a C major chord consists of the notes C, E, and G, right? C is the root, E is the third, and G is the fifth. Here's what I want you to do. With the index finger of your fingering hand, play the note C on the eighth fret of the E string. Keep the note pushed down. Now take your ring finger from the same hand and press down on the ninth fret on the G string. That note is an E. Play them both at the same time. Make sure to only play those two strings, not the two in the middle. That's what C major sounds like. All that you did was spread out the distance between the C and the E by moving the E up one octave.

When the third of a chord is played up an octave, it's called a *10th.* Why a 10th? Think back to Chapter 2, when you learned about assigning numbers to each note of the scale. Well, if you were to continue going up the scale past 8, which is the octave, 10 would be an E. Take a look at Figure 9.5.

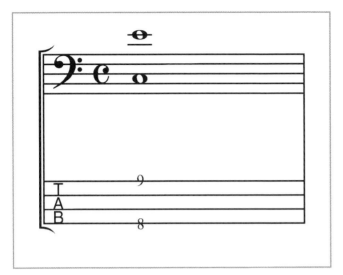

Figure 9.4
A C major double stop

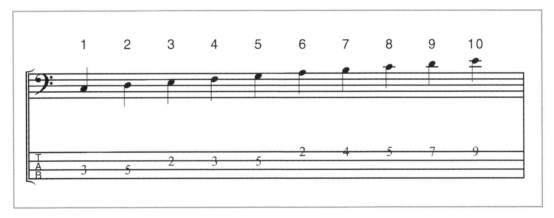

Figure 9.5
C to E, a 10th

Leave Out the Fifth

You're probably wondering what happened to the G, or fifth. For now, you're only going to be playing the root and the 10th of the chord, not the fifth. This is because the root and 10th really define the quality and sound of the chord. The fifth is implied.

Now I'll show you how to play double stops for the other two chords that we went over, F major and G major. It's easy for me to just show you the fingering and move on, but it's really important for you to know how to figure this out.

So, with that being said, let's try the F major double stop. We're trying to play the root and the major 10th, right? The root is easy; it's the F. Play an F on the first fret of the E string, again with your index finger. Now, where is that major 10th? Rather than count up 10 notes in the scale, I like to find the major third and then play it up an octave. That will give you the major 10th. So a major third up from F is A. Play the A up an octave on the second fret of the G string, using your ring finger. It's easy if you play major double stops with your index finger on the root and your ring finger on the major 10th. See Figure 9.6.

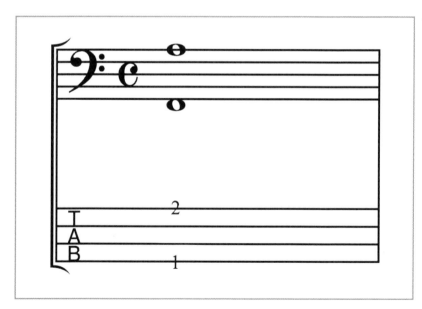

Figure 9.6
An F major double stop

What about a G major double stop? Go through the following process in your mind, as follows:

1. Find the root note. Play it on the E string with the index finger of your fingering hand.

2. Now find the major 10th. Go up a major third from G, which gives you B; now go up one octave from that. Play that B on the G string with your ring finger.

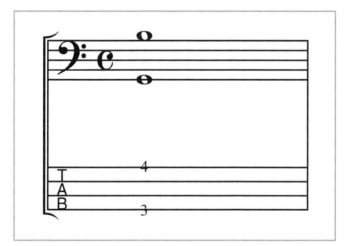

Figure 9.7
A G major double stop

Figure 9.8 shows an exercise using all three of the double stops that you just learned. Check it out.

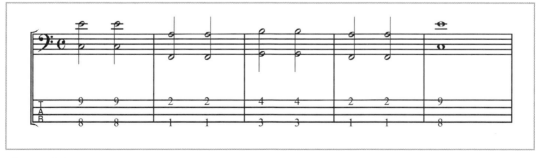

Figure 9.8
Double stop exercise in C major

Minor Double Stops

Now what about minor chords? Let's stay in the key of C major. What I want you to do is start with the note A and play the first, third, and fifth notes of the scale. That will give you the notes A, C, and E. Play them one at a time on your bass. Now think about the intervals of this chord. Notice that the distance between the first two notes, A and C, is a minor third and the distance between the second two notes C and E is a major third. See Figure 9.9.

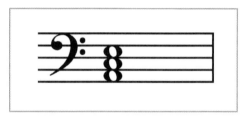

Figure 9.9
An A minor chord

How can you play a minor double stop? It's very similar to playing a major double stop, except instead of playing the root and the major 10th, you'll play the root and the minor 10th. Let's try it with A minor. Okay, so the root note is A. Play the A on the fifth fret of the E string. I like to play the root note with my middle finger for minor double stops. Now instead of going up a *major* third and raising it an octave, I want you to go up a *minor* third and raise it an octave. A minor third above A is C. The best spot to play that C up an octave is on the fifth fret of the G string. Use your ring finger. See Figure 9.10.

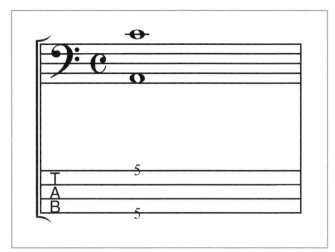

Figure 9.10
An A minor double stop

A cool thing about minor double stops is that the root and the minor 10th are played on the same fret, just on different strings. So if you can find the root on the E string, you know that the minor 10th will be on that same fret, just on the G string. Similarly, with major 10th double stops you can find the root on the E string and the 10th on the G string, but that major 10th will be one fret higher than the root. Now try playing a D minor double stop. Find the root, and then the minor 10th. Play it before you look at the example. shown in Figure 9.11

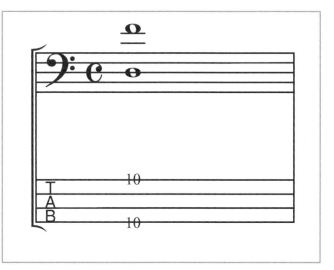

Figure 9.11
A D minor double stop

Figure 9.12 shows a song that combines major and minor double stops.

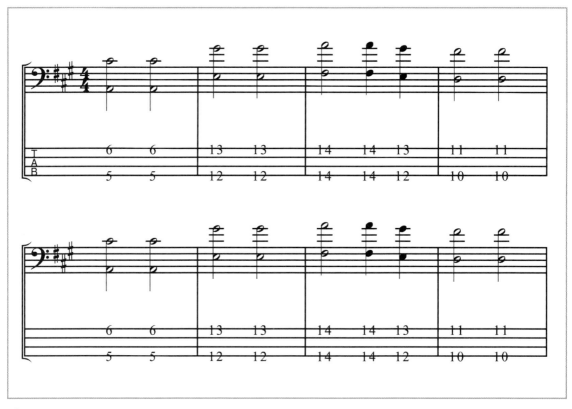

Figure 9.12
"Knights" by Knights on Earth

Which Chords Go Together?

OKAY, SO NOW THAT YOU KNOW how to play a few chords, how do you know which ones go together? The first point to realize is that every key has a group of chords that fit into it. This is all based on the scale that the key is in. For instance, in C major, there is a group of seven chords that are called the *diatonic chords.* These chords are built on each note in the C major scale, as shown in Figure 9.13.

Figure 9.13
Diatonic chords in C major

Again, notice that the key signature applies to all of the chords in the key. The key of C major has no sharps and no flats; therefore all of the chords in C major will follow that rule—no sharps, no flats. Also take note of the roman numerals below the chord names. Just like with scale degrees, numbers can be applied to chords.

The Diminished Chord

You already know about major and minor chords, but you're probably asking yourself what that *diminished* chord is all about in Figure 9.13. Let's take a moment to review the intervals between the three notes that make up major and minor chords. Starting with the root note, major chords consist of a major third, followed by a minor third. Minor chords consist of a minor third, followed by a major third. Diminished chords sound totally different because they are constructed of two minor thirds. Take a look at Figure 9.14.

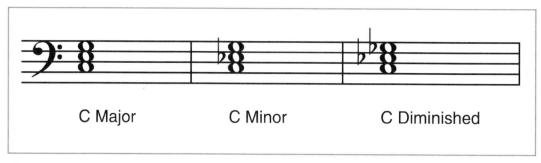

Figure 9.14
Intervals of major, minor, and diminished chords

Play through each chord on your bass, one note at a time. You'll hear that while major chords sound happy and minor chords sound sad, diminished chords sound totally unstable, almost creepy. Take note that the seventh chord of all major scales is always diminished. Refer back to Figure 9.13 to see the diminished chord in the key of C major.

Playing Major Scales in 10ths

THE LAST THING THAT I WANT you to do is to play double stops for all seven notes in the scale. It's like you're playing a major scale, but with 10ths. I'll walk you through it in G major.

Figure 9.15
G major scale in 10ths

This is a sound that's very important to familiarize yourself with. Once you have a grasp of where all of the double stops are, I want you to mix up the order. Play them up and down until you barely have to think about it anymore. Just play around in the key of G and come up with an order that sounds good to you. Once you feel like you've mastered the key of G, try doing it in A major, or any other key.

Closing Thoughts

YOU'VE LEARNED QUITE A LOT in the past nine chapters. You should now have a pretty basic understanding of note names, scales, reading music, ear training, harmony, and even some specialty bass techniques. Remember that these lessons take time to digest. As you know, bass isn't a skill you pick up overnight; it's a craft that requires sculpting. I have been thinking about and practicing bass for 15 years now, and there's still so much to work on. That's one of the greatest things about music; it's endless. There's always more to do.

Figure 9.16
Bass is a skill that requires developing; have fun!

With that being said, I want you to know that I chose the topics in this book because I feel that they help create a musical foundation that is relevant to all types of music. The concepts covered in this book will help you regardless of the musical path you choose. So follow whatever interests you, whether it's rock, jazz, classical, funk, pop, or some style or genre that doesn't exist yet. Maybe you like all of those styles; maybe none of them. It's completely up to you. Have fun with it!

Great

Bass Players

ONE OF THE BEST WAYS to become better at the bass is to listen to great bass players. Obviously there are tons of amazing bass players out there, and it's impossible to check out all of them, but there are some people whom I think everyone should hear. This is my list of the top 20 most influential bass players. I can honestly say that everyone on this list has changed the way that I think about playing bass. I promise you that these people are worth listening to. In my mind, these are the masters. In no particular order, here they are:

- ▶ **Paul McCartney with The Beatles**
- ▶ **Pino Palladino with The Who, John Mayer, and Tears For Fears**
- ▶ **Tony Levin with Peter Gabriel**
- ▶ **Rick Danko with The Band**
- ▶ **Sting with The Police**
- ▶ **James Jamerson with Stevie Wonder and on hundreds of Motown recordings**

- Les Claypool with Primus
- Colin Greenwood with Radiohead
- Larry Graham with Sly and the Family Stone
- Flea with The Red Hot Chili Peppers
- Bootsy Collins with James Brown and Parliament Funkadelic
- Victor Wooten with Bela Fleck and the Flecktones
- Jaco Pastorius as a solo artist
- MeShell N'degeocello as a solo artist
- John Paul Jones with Led Zeppelin
- Kaveh Rastegar with Kneebody
- Skuli Sverisson with Ben Monder and Alan Holdsworth
- Rhonda Smith with Prince
- Richard Bona as a solo artist
- John Patitucci as a solo artist

B

Glossary

T HIS GLOSSARY CONTAINS all the important terms and concepts discussed throughout the book. The point is to bring them all in one convenient area, so you can look up terms as you need to and review anything you've forgotten or don't understand.

12-Bar Blues Form

The earliest blues music didn't necessarily have a standard measure or bar length until around the 1930s. This is when the 12-bar blues became the standard. ("12-bar" refers to the amount of measures that it takes to complete this blues pattern.) This blues form can be played in any key and only uses three chords.

Accidental

A notation symbol that is used to lower (as a flat does) or raise (as a sharp does) the pitch of a note. Sharps raise the pitch of a note by one half step, or one fret, whereas flats lower the pitch of a note by one half step, or one fret. (See also "Flat" and "Sharp".)

The Bass Clef

This is the symbol located all the way to the left of the staff that determines the pitch of written notes. Because you aspire to be a bass player, you'll be reading the bass clef. Some other instruments that share the bass clef are the trombone, cello, and tuba. Notes written in bass clef are much lower in pitch than notes written in treble clef (which contains many notes that are too high to be played on a bass guitar). See Figure B.1.

Figure B.1
The bass and treble clefs

The Blues Scale

One main characteristic of blues music is the use of *blue notes.* Blue notes refer to the lowering of the third, fifth, and seventh degrees of a scale by a half step. Figure B.2 shows a blues scale written out in the key of G.

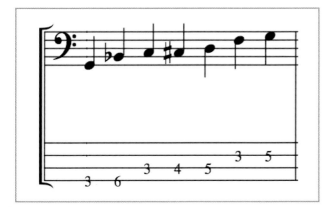

Figure B.2
Blues scale written out in the key of G

Chord

When three or more notes are played at the same time.

Circle of Fifths

In music, you have a total of 12 keys: C, G, D, A, E, B, F♯/G♭, C♯/D♭, A♭, E♭, B♭, and F. This pattern of notes is called the *circle of fifths.* Each of these keys has a different number of sharp or flat notes, and the circle of fifths is a really easy way of memorizing them. It's called the *circle of fifths* because there are five notes between each key.

The circle of fifths can help you determine how many sharps or flats there are in a specific key or scale. The numbers inside the circle refer to the number of sharps or flats in that major scale. So for instance, the D major scale has two sharps, as shown in Figure B.3. Figure B.4 shows the circle of fifths with minor keys.

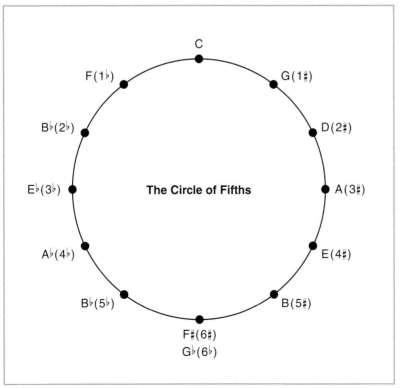

Figure B.3
The circle of fifths

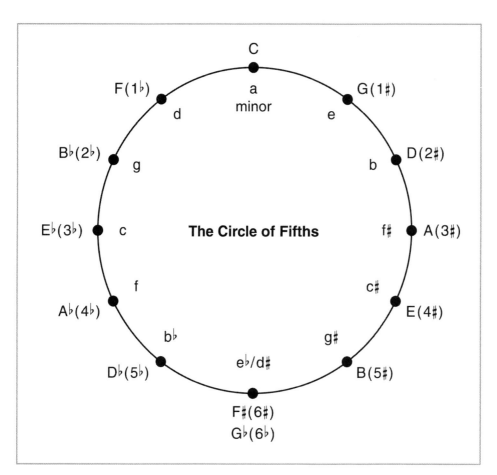

Figure B.4
The circle of fifths with minor keys

Diminished Chord

A chord that has a diminished fifth in it. More specifically, it is a diminished triad consisting of a minor third and a diminished fifth above the root—if built on C, a diminished chord would have a C, an E♭, and a G♭. The interval between the upper two notes is also a minor third—thus, the chord consists of two minor thirds stacked on top of one another. It resembles a minor triad with a lowered (or diminished) fifth.

Fingerboard

The fingerboard (also known as a fretboard) is the long, thin strip of wood that is laminated to the front of the neck of the bass. You press down on the fingerboard frets when you play the bass, which changes the pitch of the strings and is called "stopping" the strings.

Fingering Hand

This is the hand you use to press down the notes on the fingerboard of the bass. If you are right-handed, your left hand is the fingering hand. Remember these important notes about your fingering hand:

▶ **Line your thumb up with your middle finger (so your hand acts as a clamp).**

▶ **Play with the tips of your fingers.**

▶ **Avoid sharp wrist angles.**

(See also "Plucking Hand".)

Flat (♭)

An accidental that lowers the pitch of a note by one half step, or one fret.

Fret

The raised ridge on the neck of the bass; it extends generally across the full width of the neck. The fret divides the neck into fixed segments—each fret represents one semitone.

Half Step

A major scale is made up of a combination of *whole steps* and *half steps*. A whole step is an interval of two semitones, and a half step is an interval of one semitone. A whole step is the distance between two frets on your bass and a half step is the distance between one. (Recall that a *semitone* is the distance between one fret.)

Hammering

Part of the slap bass technique, also often called a hammer-on. This technique can bring your slapping to a whole new level, and it's easy. After slapping an open string, you push down on the fret with your fingering hand. So you're slapping the string once, and getting two notes to sound, one right after the other. (See also "Slap Bass".)

Harmonic

A technique whereby you pluck a note, and then take your finger off of the fret. The note should ring for a while and will have a "bell-like" tone, which is called a harmonic.

Humbucker Pickup Configuration

A more rare bass pickup, the *humbucker* is similar in length to the jazz-style pickup but is roughly double the width. These types of pickups are usually found in newer, more modern-sounding basses and tend to be louder than a standard jazz or precision pickup. (See "Pickup Configuration" for more information.)

Interval

The difference in pitch between two notes. Each note in a scale can be given a number—C=1, D=2, E=3, F=4, and so on—as shown in Figure B.5.

The distance between the notes C and D is called a major second. When you're trying to determine the interval between two notes, count the number of scale steps between them, starting with 1 for the lowest note. If you have G and D for instance, the number of scale degrees between them is five (G, A, B, C, D), making the interval a fifth.

Figure B.5
C major scale with assigned numbers

Key Signature

A key signature is always placed right after the clef, and tells you the key of the music you're reading. The key signature will display the sharps or flats in the appropriate order. When you see that a sharp or a flat is written in a specific space or line in a key signature, it means that every note that is played in that line or space will be sharp or flat. So if you see a B♭ in the key signature, all it means is that every time that you see a B written in the music you should actually play a B♭.

Ledger Line

The line you see written through a note on a staff. Ledger lines are used to extend the staff and are used for notes that are really high or really low (see Figure B.6).

Figure B.6
Ledger lines

Measure

A rhythmic grouping of notes that contains a fixed number of beats; in notated music, it falls between the vertical bar lines on a staff. (See also "Time Signature".)

Mode

A *mode* is a type of scale. Just like a major or a minor scale, modes have seven different notes. There are seven modes in total, and each mode has a different sound or tonal structure. They are Ionian, Dorian, Phrygian, Lydian, Mixolydian, Aeolian, and Locrian.

Open String

When you play a string without pushing down a fret.

Pickup Configuration

The pickup configuration captures the vibrations of the strings and sends those vibrations to your amplifier and has a huge impact on the sound of the bass. Some common bass pickup types are precision, or "P," pickups and jazz, or "J," pickups. A "P" pickup configuration (displayed in Figure B.7) consists of two small pickups offset slightly along the length of the body of the bass. Notice that each pickup is placed beneath two strings.

Figure B.7
The "P" pickup configuration

The "J" pickup configuration (displayed in Figure B.8) consists of two longer pickups that are spaced farther apart. The pickup closest to the bridge of the bass is referred to as the *bridge* or *back* pickup. The pickup closest to the neck of the bass is referred to as the *neck* or the *front* pickup. Notice that each "J" pickup spans all four strings of the bass, while each "P" pickup spans across two strings.

Figure B.8
The "J" pickup configuration

Generally, P-style pickups are used in rock music and J-style pickups are used in jazz or fusion music. However, this rule is broken all the time. Plenty of rock bass players use jazz-style pickups, and although it is a little less common, there are jazz players who use P-style pickups. The best way to figure out which sound you prefer is to try both types. There is no wrong or right decision when it comes to pickups; it's all personal preference. Some basses even come with both types of pickups.

Plucking Hand

This is the hand that you pluck the strings with. If you are right-handed, your right hand is the plucking hand. Plucking close to the bridge gives you a clear, defined sound, whereas plucking close to the neck gives you a warm, round sound.

Remember these important notes about your plucking hand:

▶ **Mute the strings that are not being played.**

▶ **Alternate your fingers when plucking.**

▶ **Keep your pinky down.**

▶ **Keep your wrist straight.**

(See also "Fingering Hand".)

Semitone

The distance of one fret.

Sharp (♯)

An accidental that raises the pitch of a note by one half step, or one fret.

Slap Bass

A percussive technique that consists of two actions: using the side of your thumb to hit the strings of the bass (slapping) and snapping the strings with your middle or index finger (popping). Both are done with your plucking hand. Think of the slaps as bass drum hits and the pops as snare drum hits. This style of playing was developed, and for the most part introduced, by a bass player named Larry Graham. Slapping is most common in funk and pop music. (See also "Hammering".)

The Staff

A set of five horizontal lines, as illustrated in Figure B.9. Notes are placed in different locations on the staff to indicate different pitches. A staff is read from left to right, just like a book. The height of the note determines its pitch. The higher the note is placed on the staff, the higher it will be in pitch. The lower the note is placed on the staff, the lower it will be in pitch.

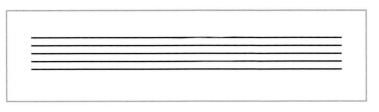

Figure B.9
The staff

Tablature

An easy way to read music—see Figure B.10. The four lines that you see represent the four strings of the bass from the lowest to the highest. The numbers shown on the strings tell you which fret to play. For instance, a number three on the lowest line means you play the third fret on the E, or lowest, string.

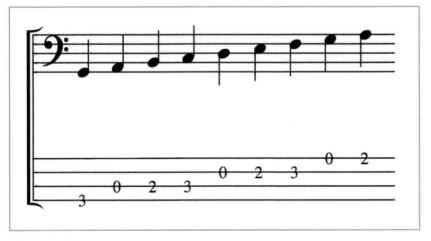

Figure B.10
Notes on the staff with tablature

Tapping

A technique where the bass player taps the strings against the fretboard to get a sound. This can be done with the fingering hand or the plucking hand. It's as if the player is treating the bass like a piano. You don't pluck the note with one hand and finger it with the other; you do both with the same hand.

Thumb, Hammer, Pluck Technique

This technique was developed by Victor Wooten. The basic idea is that the bass player slaps a note with the thumb of the plucking hand, hammers a note with the fingering hand, and pops or "plucks" a note with the plucking hand. Once you learn the coordination, you can apply any notes that you like.

Time Signature

Relates to the timing of the music that you're reading and tells you how many and what kind of notes are in each measure. (A *measure* indicates the total number of notes or rests between two bar lines.) See Figure B.11.

Figure B.11
Time signature of 4/4 (four quarter notes in each measure)

There are two numbers that make up a time signature. The top number tells you how many notes of a certain kind there are in each measure and the bottom number tells you what kind of notes the top line is referring to. The most common time signatures are 4/4 (common time), 2/4 (cut time), and 3/4.

Tritone

An interval that used to be called "the devil in music" for its evil-sounding quality. This goes back to the 18th century, when members of the church would be punished for singing a tritone. The tritone consists of three whole steps. In the key of C, the tritone would be F♯. Figure B.12 shows this tritone.

Figure B.12
The tritone, sometimes called "the devil in music"

Watts

A watt refers to electrical power. The higher the wattage, the more power an amp has. More power equals more volume. A 15- to 30-watt amp is ideal for practicing alone in your room. A 50-watt amp produces enough power or volume to start playing with a band in a small venue. An amp with 200–500 watts is used for bigger situations, such as playing in a club in front of a few hundred people.

Whole Step

A major scale is made up of a combination of *whole steps* and *half steps*. A whole step is an interval of two semitones, and a half step is an interval of one semitone. A whole step is the distance between two frets on your bass and a half step is the distance of one. (Recall that a *semitone* is the distance of one fret.)

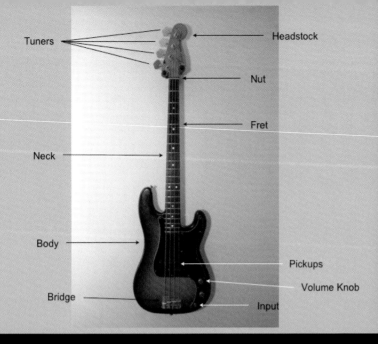

Tuners

Headstock

Nut

Fret

Neck

Body

Pickups

Volume Knob

Bridge

Input

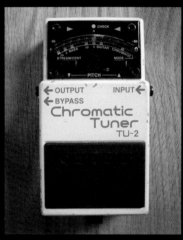

Chromatic
Tuner
TU-2

OUTPUT   INPUT

BYPASS

Index

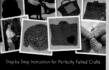